Insurrections

ALSO AVAILABLE FROM BLOOMSBURY

Pedagogy of Resistance, *Henry A. Giroux*
Critical Pedagogy and the Covid-19 Pandemic,
    edited by Fatma Mizikaci and Eda Ata
Capitalism, Pedagogy, and the Politics of Being, *Noah DeLissovoy*
Ecopedagogy, *Greg William Misiaszek*
Transnational Feminist Politics, Education, and Social Justice,
    edited by Silvia Edling and Sheila Macrine
Race, Politics, and Pandemic Pedagogy, *Henry A. Giroux*
Education, Equality and Justice in the New Normal,
    edited by Inny Accioly and Donaldo Macedo
On Critical Pedagogy, 2nd edition, *Henry A. Giroux*
Pedagogy of Hope, *Paulo Freire*
Pedagogy of the Heart, *Paulo Freire*
Pedagogy in Process, *Paulo Freire*
Education for Critical Consciousness, *Paulo Freire*
Paulo Freire: A Philosophical Biography, *Walter Omar Kohan*
Education for Social Change, *Douglas Bourn*

Insurrections

Education in an Age of Counter-Revolutionary Politics

HENRY A. GIROUX

BLOOMSBURY ACADEMIC
LONDON · NEW YORK · OXFORD · NEW DELHI · SYDNEY

BLOOMSBURY ACADEMIC
Bloomsbury Publishing Plc
50 Bedford Square, London, WC1B 3DP, UK
1385 Broadway, New York, NY 10018, USA
29 Earlsfort Terrace, Dublin 2, Ireland

BLOOMSBURY, BLOOMSBURY ACADEMIC and the Diana logo
are trademarks of Bloomsbury Publishing Plc

First published in Great Britain 2023

A catalogue record for this book is available from the British Library.

A catalog record for this book is available from the Library of Congress.

ISBN: HB: 978-1-3503-5082-3
         PB: 978-1-3503-5081-6
         ePDF: 978-1-3503-5083-0
         eBook: 978-1-3503-5084-7

Typeset by Integra Software Services Pvt. Ltd.
Printed and bound in Great Britain

To find out more about our authors and books visit www.bloomsbury.com
and sign up for our newsletters.

For Rania—who is always there for me,
especially in the most difficult times.
For Robin D. G. Kelley—whose brilliance is only matched
by his courage.
For Noam Chomsky—who never stopped making
power accountable and resistance essential.
For Donaldo Macedo—my brother for over forty-five years who
always reminded me that the longing for justice was
inseparable from the longing for solidarity.

No history is mute. No matter how much they own it, break it, and lie about it, human history refuses to shut its mouth. Despite deafness and ignorance, the time that was continues to tick inside the time that is.

—EDUARDO GALEANO

The whole of history is about hopes being sustained, lost and renewed.

—JOHN BERGER

I am generally very alone… Not exactly alone. But not really present.

—JAMES BALDWIN

CONTENTS

ACKNOWLEDGMENTS

I am grateful to Mark Richardson at Bloomsbury for continuing to support my work.

My wife, Rania, read every page and often pushed me in directions I never imagined, illustrating relentlessly her brilliance and support. She continues to be the force that holds my life together and brings me, to quote Pablo Neruda, an "implacable sweetness." My former assistant Maya Sabados once again did an excellent job reading and editing the manuscript with each new update. Thanks to Robin Goodman for the excellent job in editing the text. I am thankful and appreciative for the support given to me by a number of dear friends, including Donaldo Macedo, Rowan Wolf, Jasmin Habib, Ken Saltman, Gustavo Figueiredo, Tony Penna, Brad Evans, Sheila Macrine, Robin D. G. Kelley, Dean Birkenkamp, Oscar Zambrano, Tony DiMaggio, Paul Street, Christopher Robbins, and Alex Means. I also want to thank a number of close associates who publish my work: Maya Schenwar and Alana Price at *Truthout*, Michael Lerner at *Tikkun*, Jeffrey St. Clair at *Counterpunch*, Rowan Wolf at *Uncommon Thought*, David M. Arditi at *Fast Capitalism*, and Andrew O'Hehir at *Salon*. Thanks to *Rise Up Times*, which has reprinted much of my work and to which I am deeply grateful. Over the years a number of editors, especially Dean Birkenkamp and Jane Fargnoli stuck by me with encouragement and support that was quite extraordinary. It has been a hard few years with the passing of a number of my intellectual heroes and mentors, which included Stanley Aronowitz, Zygmunt Bauman, and Keith Tester. A number of the ideas in this book appeared in different forms in *Truthout, Counterpunch, Salon*, and the *Review of Education, Pedagogy, and Cultural Studies*.

PART ONE

Politics in an Age of Counter-Revolution

CHAPTER ONE

Introduction

The future of democracy in the United States will not be determined by the malignant decisions made by a reactionary group of Supreme Court justices who are waging a war on the most fundamental elements of democracy.[1] Nor will it be decided by the existence of voter suppression laws, the ubiquity of the "big lie" massive structural inequality, or the rise of white nationalism and a politics dominated by white supremacist ideology. Neither will it be decided by the rhetorical accelerant endlessly produced by former President Trump with his frequent allusions to violence and armed revolt.[2] It will not be determined by a Republican Party that wages war on transgender youth, women, and people of color or a Democratic Party wedded to a savagely cruel neoliberal capitalism.

The destruction of democracy and its institutions will result from the increasing attack on ethical standards, the undermining of truth, and a mass consciousness that supports violence as a central weapon for social change. Accelerating this breakdown of democracy is the disabling of memory, the mass production of ignorance, and the weakening of the collective imagination. To the degree that the public can be convinced, as Judith Butler argues, that the "call for democracy is interpreted as sedition [and] the call for freedom is taken to be a call to violence," democracy will suffer from a legitimation crisis and will disintegrate.[3] Under these conditions, the devastation produced by capitalism will accelerate and become normalized; moreover, state-sponsored punishment will expand and will be used to criminalize more and more social problems; increasingly, fascist politics will gain more legitimacy and potentially prevail in the United States.

Since the brutal attack on the Capitol on January 6, insurrection has become a dominant motif informing politics, social media, and the mainstream press. Recurring images of the attack by a violent mob of Trump followers have solidified into a horrifying epic of lawlessness and deadly assaults, adding a ruthless optic to a long history of white supremacy, American exceptionalism, gangster capitalism, and state violence.[4] All of which was amplified by the House Jan. 6 committee hearings, which provided a civics lesson on a resurgent authoritarianism and white nationalism at work in the United States. While the mainstream media have failed to see the signs, authoritarianism's historical political, racial, and cultural dynamics have become more visible, taking on a seditious and coarsening reality as they have emerged in boldly rhetorical, increasingly violent, and terrifying forms. Part spectacle, part reality check, the images of violence on January 6 have been appropriated not only by those exposing the dark side of authoritarianism but also by those, such as Rep. Marjorie Taylor Greene, who view the event as a symbol of what they term "our 1776 moment."[5]

Images associated with the Capitol insurrection included the waving of Confederate flags, "a makeshift wooden gallows, with stairs and a rope erected on the Mall," "Camp Auschwitz" shirts, a sea of MAGA hats, and a frenzied crowd with some people yelling "Hang Mike Pence!" "Shoot the politicians," "Fight for Trump," and "America first!"—a "phrase popularized in 1940 by Nazi sympathizers" in the United States.[6] Videos and TV footage of Capitol and DC police officers being attacked, beaten, and pummeled—over 140 were injured—revealed a vicious mob that believed it was above the law, urged on by Trump at a rally earlier that day, in which he stated, "If you don't fight like hell, you're not going to have a country anymore."[7] These were not innocent words said unintentionally in the heat of the moment. The impact of his incitement has to be measured against a range of comments provoking violence that Trump made in previous speeches and rallies. As Fabiola Cineas reported in *Vox*:

> Trump's messaging on January 6 is precisely in line with how he's historically addressed violence on the part of hate groups and his supporters: He emboldens it. As far back as 2015, Trump has been connected to documented acts of violence, with perpetrators claiming that he was even their inspiration. In fact, dozens of

people enacted violence in Trump's name in the years before the Capitol attack, according to a 2020 report from ABC News.[8]

Trump's attack on the foundations of democratic rule received enormous legitimation from his base and political party, and it was deeply rooted in a culture that normalized violence as a political tool while becoming increasingly cruel, frighteningly intolerant, and unabashedly disdainful of democracy. Even more disturbing is how Trump's lies, racism, and attacks on his enemies attracted a broad swath of individuals of different ages and occupations, living in different parts of the country. Nowhere was the mainstreaming of radical politics more evident than in the fact that right-wing extremist groups such as anti-government militia could recruit both young and older people and create "a network across the US that include[d] former military members, police and border patrol agents."[9] Some of the individuals who attacked the Capitol police were still serving in the US military.

This dehumanizing reality did not begin with the Trump presidency. His recharging of white supremacist ideology and its merging with the discourse of violence has, as Henry Louis Gates, Jr. observes, "a long tradition and it's a legacy of the rollback to Reconstruction."[10] Trump's success in mobilizing millions to support his lies, racism, and unmitigated disrespect for the law has resuscitated terrifying elements in the social order that were once relegated to its margins. This flourishing reactionary political formation comes not only from the powerful influence of a right-wing propaganda machine and structural anti-democratic features built into the American political system—including the Electoral College, the filibuster, and the role of money in determining electoral outcomes—it is also the result of the Republican Party's willingness to embrace unabashed white supremacy and a rebranded form of fascism as a gateway to power.[11]

How else to explain Trump's willingness to publicly make overtly racist comments as part of his broader attempt to expand his political power and gain more adherents to his evidence-free claim about a stolen election. Throughout his presidency and beyond, Trump has stirred racial tensions by mobilizing notions of white grievance.[12] In the aftermath of the Biden election, Trump has done more than falsely claim the other side stole the election, reinforcing a dangerous strain of racism; he has also endorsed "white replacement theory" with his lie about whites being shortchanged by people of color. White replacement theory is a core ideology of white supremacists, who falsely claim that people of color are jeopardizing, if not replacing, the power, privileges, livelihoods, and rights of white people.[13] For instance, at a political rally in Texas, Trump went so far as to claim that he was a victim of racism, as are white people in general. He told a Saturday night rally in Florence, Arizona, in January 2022 that "The left is now rationing lifesaving therapeutics based on race, discriminating against and denigrating ... white people to determine who lives and who dies. If you're white you don't get the vaccine, or if you're white, you don't get therapeutics ... In New York State, if you're white, you have to go to the back of the line to get medical health."[14] White replacement theory has become code for racial cleansing and racial purity, parading under "frantic appeals to white survivalism."[15] While white replacement theory has a long history in the United States and Europe, it has taken on a new urgency given its compatibility with a growing fascist politics and militant white nationalism. It has become a central tenet of the modern Republican Party, which argues that white people as an alleged "native population" are being replaced by undocumented immigrants, Muslims, and others considered outside of the acceptable parameters of whiteness. Moreover, it is increasingly supported by prominent Republican officials, pundits, and media celebrities such as Fox News' Tucker Carlson.[16]

A week after Trump's poisonous racist lie, close to two dozen white nationalists took Trump's incendiary racist comments seriously and protested in front of Brigham and Women's Hospital in Boston, holding a bedsheet with black lettering reading "B and W Hospital Kills Whites."[17] The line between Trump's racist rhetoric and his open display of fascism is too direct to be ignored. Trump is not alone on the global stage. "Authoritarians are on the march" once again in Brazil, India, Hungary, Turkey, and Russia, and "in a disturbingly long list of other countries."[18]

Racism has once again become a central pillar of a political party, becoming a mark of pride, bigotry, and virtue. Democracy has reached a dangerous point and is once again under siege on a global level. As the Economist Intelligence Unit observed at the beginning of 2022, less than half the world is living in a democracy, and only "6.4 percent live in a full democracy."[19] Freedom House also released a report stating that democracy is in retreat worldwide. What is unique about *Freedom in the World 2022* is that it singles out the United States, specifically Trump and the Republican Party, for the suppression of voting rights, attempts to overturn the election, and the ongoing sabotage of American democracy.[20]

Equally disturbing is that the promises and ideals of democracy are being replaced by a fascist politics that trades in deeply authoritarian principles. These include racial discrimination, censorship, widespread disinformation, xenophobic nationalism, suppression of dissent, the threat and use of violence to achieve political ends, the conflation of state and corporate power, the cult of personality, a culture of fear and cruelty, white supremacy, and the absolute veneration of the strongman. The display of overt white supremacy by Republican Trump loyalists in the confirmation hearings of the well-respected Judge Ketanji Brown Jackson was an "object lesson for the entire world on the ongoing dynamics of systemic racism in the United States."[21] She endured a range of nauseating racist attacks by six right-wing GOP Senators in which she was accused of being soft on sentencing child pornographers, interrogated about her alleged support for the evils of critical race theory, and harangued over the revealing issue of whether she believed interracial marriage should have been left to the states, all of which had "little to do with the actual work of the supreme court."[22] As Jack Ahern pointed out in *Salon*, "White supremacy was undergirding each and every one of these senator's questions, far exceeding the level of mere dog-whistles."[23] Racism has now become political theater—a performative act of unhinged bigotry and moral degradation. We have seen these trends before in times much darker than the present.

Attacks on democracy via threats of violence are hallmarks of fascist and authoritarian politics. This was clear not only in Mussolini's use of Blackshirts to intimidate his opponents but also in Hitler's use of his voluntary paramilitary force, the Brownshirts, which attacked Jews, gays, leftists, and other critics of Nazi ideology. Both groups have their contemporary American counterparts not only in groups such as the Proud Boys, Oath Keepers, and Three Percenters but also in far-right politicians such as Paul Gosar, Marjorie Taylor Greene, Matt Gaetz, and Lauren Boebert and spokespersons including Steve Bannon, Michael Flynn, Roger Stone, and Tucker Carlson. The terror of the unforeseen and unthinkable that runs through history—at work currently in Orbán's Hungary, Marcos Jr.'s Philippines, Bolsonaro's Brazil,

Putin's Russia, and Modi's India, among other countries—is with us once again, rekindling violence, fear, and bigotry while offering the American public the swindle of fulfillment at work in the emotionally charged, hate-filled, conspiracy laden appeal of a rebranded populist form of neoliberal fascism. The callousness of neoliberalism has found its most powerful form of legitimation in the claim that the only alternative to its own failures is the call to replace the idea of democracy with the promises of an illiberal democracy—twenty-first century code for white nationalism, white supremacy, and unchecked authoritarianism.

CHAPTER TWO

Necropolitics and the Politics of White Nationalism

The violent assaults against humanity seem to never cease. As Brad Evans notes, "Humanity is bound to the sacrificial model of existence."[1] Americans are once again deaf to the silent screams of the victims, the disappeared, the abducted, and the tortured. The monstrous tyrannies of history are no longer frozen in the past and now inform the present. The spirit of counter-revolution in fascist discourse, policies, and threats is with us again and can be seen in growing support for bigotry and white nationalism among the Republican Party and their base, buttressed by the increased presence of armed militia and an increasingly well-armed populace.[2]

Within the current abysmal historical moment, a mix of aggrieved agency, a tsunami of conspiracy theories, and an expanding culture of lies fuels a massive political effort to legitimate and normalize white minority rule. Underlying this authoritarian political project is a massive ideological scaffolding reproducing the lethal workings of repressive power. Cultural pathways that solidify the identities and legitimate the agents willing to embrace a political landscape of fascist agitation and violence are enabled by this project. This is a pedagogical effort and attack, the aim of which is to refute elements of the past as a site of injustice, enable a machinery of exclusion and disposability, and build an apparatus of racial cleansing, exclusion, and disposability wedded to what Kimberlé Williams Crenshaw calls "The Unmattering of Black lives."[3]

Talk of civil war has emerged at a time when violence has become a powerful force for shaping language and addressing social problems, and it is emerging as a central organizing principle of politics. Central to this brutalizing of civic culture and the social imagination is the need to acknowledge that long before violence becomes normalized in society, politics descends into what John Berger once called ethicide—a cultural logic composed of "agents [who] kill ethics and therefore any notion of history and justice."[4] At work here is a collective disavowal of social responsibility and the removal of political, discursive, and economic actions from any sense of the social costs involved. Central to the turn toward ethicide is a Republican Party waging a counter-revolution against the foundations of democratic rule.

This is a right-wing political party wedded to a politics of dehumanization, social amnesia, social abandonment, and terminal exclusion—a party strongly committed to the acceleration of the death of the unwanted. Hints of this necropolitical project are evident in a spate of right-wing Supreme Court decisions that included rescinding a woman's constitutional right to an abortion; subverting a state's right to do background checks on individuals carrying concealed weapons; diminishing the power of the government to address climate change; eviscerating the line separating church and state; and weakening the 1965 Voting rights Act. Under such circumstances, ethical boundaries dissolve, language is emptied of critical referents, zones of social abandonment become normalized, racial purity is embraced, historical amnesia is celebrated, and a culture of violence becomes commonplace. Ethicide emerges from the mechanisms of cultural politics via education, social media, militarization, spectacularized propaganda performances, and the false promises of demagogues. As Amee Vanderpool observes, a docile public plagued by anger, racism, and ignorance is now the object of right-wing politicians who use their propagandistic skills and media savvy "to channel and convert anger and fear into a shield and a weapon."[5] Under such circumstances, individuals remove their actions from any sense of personal responsibility, fall under the spell of cult leaders, abandon their role as critical agents, and blindly inhabit the discourse of white supremacy while prioritizing violence as a political tool.

Right-wing extremists in the Republican Party and their popular base have embraced violence in both symbolic and concrete terms.

This has taken place historically in the United States at a moment when blood flows freely at the borders, on poor neighborhood streets, and in back alleys, detention centers, prisons, schools, and other sites where violence reaches into all the spaces that make up daily life. Mass shootings, gun violence, police violence, and right-wing assaults occur daily in the ongoing war against immigrants, journalists, Black and Brown youth, school board members, and elected officials. The increasingly diverse landscape of the United States, extending from synagogues and malls to the southern border and public schools, has been touched by a culture soaked in blood. Every domain of American life from the worlds of politics and business to the arts and entertainment industries either trade in violence for profits or celebrate it as an essential response to pressing political and social problems. Violence has been spectacularized as a mode of pleasure and inhabited as a mark of national identity.

Images of Will Smith slapping Chris Rock at the Oscar ceremony dominated the mainstream press for a week, overtaking news about a much more serious issue regarding a seven-hour gap in Donald Trump's phone logs on the day of the insurrection. In this case, spectacularized violence won out over a potentially serious case of Trump "using the leverage of the violent insurrection" in order to influence Pence "to complete the procedural coup" that would overturn Biden's election.[6]

In the aftermath of the mass violence in which a hate-filled, self-proclaimed white supremacist killed ten Black people in a supermarket in Buffalo, New York, followed soon afterwards by a mass shooting in which a troubled 18-year-old, using semiautomatic firearms, shot his grandmother and then gunned down nineteen fourth graders and two teachers, the mainstream media ignored the underlying causes of the killings, focusing mostly on the personalities of the shooters and the grief of those parents and families affected by the shootings. Violence has become so normalized in America that both stories largely disappeared from the media within a few weeks.

Toni Morrison has remarked that the prevailing cultural narrative of neoliberalism and its underlying fascist politics "is recognizable by its need to purge, [and] its terror of democratic agendas."[7] "It produces perfect capitalists" largely defined as consumers, who are indifferent to ethics and more than willing to criminalize and pathologize the enemy, reward mindlessness, and maintain, at all costs, silence.[8] Morrison's insights are all the more relevant in an age when the lines between democracy and authoritarianism are collapsing. Her warning necessitates heightened critical vigilance at a moment when the culture is shifting, new political formations are emerging, and new identities are being produced. This is particularly true given the regressive pedagogical narratives that have been at work in producing the agents involved in the current attacks on democratic institutions, policies, and laws. This is a logic rooted in hate, bigotry, and cruelty, infused with a spirit of vigilante violence. Far removed from democratic values, it has provided the language and political signposts to support the attack on the Capitol, and further attacks on women's reproductive rights, voting rights, and racial justice as part of a broader effort to successfully display its affirmation and merging of politics, white nationalism, imperialism, and violence. In addition to these policies, this emerging cultural machinery has forecast the "bald political calculus" of a rising uniquely American authoritarianism.[9]

The assault on the Capitol cannot be understood merely as a unique or isolated expression of Trumpian-inspired violence. As the U.S. House Select Committee investigation of the January 6 attack on the Capitol clearly demonstrated, there is overwhelming evidence that the former president's claim of a stolen election was the animating cause of the attempted coup, and that he and other high-ranking members of his party were criminally responsible for the murderous violence that took place.[10] Moreover, they had plotted before the attack on the capital to engage in a larger coup aimed at undermining both the 2020 presidential election results and whatever was left of American democracy. Trump and his political allies made a mockery of the law by trying to pressure the justice department, state officials, Vice President Pence, election officials. and others into aiding his goal of reversing Biden's election.[11] Trump and his corrupt cohorts in the Republican Party did more than engage in seditions conspiracy, they normalized crime, corruption, state terrorism, fraud, lies, and violence.

The rise of Trumpism and the violent assault on the Capitol result from years of anti-democratic efforts by white nationalists, the financial elite, reactionary think tanks such as the Heritage Foundation, neoliberal politicians, right-wing social media, and a conservative-dominated Supreme Court. The coup attempt on January 6 was an expression of violence that has manifested itself as an organizing force of the present but has a deep resonance with the past. This contemporary expression of violence has a long history grounded in what Achille Mbembe has called necropolitics, or the politics of death—an upgraded species of fascist politics that defines whose lives are worthy of human value, citizenship, and occupying the public sphere, and, more specifically, who is considered disposable and excess.[12]

American legal scholar Lawrence Tribe rightly observes that Trump's Republican Party not only backed the attack on the Capitol but also supported a governing form "that almost always comes wrapped in violence" and is endemic to fascism.[13] How else to explain the threats and "murderous violence" by Trump's followers aimed at school board members who support pupils wearing masks, medical personnel who support lockdowns, election officials who refuse the lie of fraudulent elections, and politicians who dare to disagree with Trump's policies.[14] The political scientist Robert A. Pape argues that a new politically violent mass movement has developed to restore the Trump presidency. This includes "21 million adamant supporters of insurrection [who] have the dangerous potential for violent mobilization" and are willing to shed bloodshed for their cause.[15]

What are we to make, for that matter, of Republican Governor Ron DeSantis signing legislation "that gives legal protections to people who drive their cars into protesters in the street" and defines as criminal felons individuals who "while protesting break a window or engage in other alleged illegal activity."[16] As Thom Hartmann rightly observes: "With DeSantis and other Republican governors pre-exonerating people like the driver who viciously killed Heather Heyer and vigilante protest shooters like [Kyle] Rittenhouse, many are worried that we're entering a new era where vigilante shooters and drivers-into-crowds will become as normalized and accepted as ... daily mass shootings have become in America."[17]

This authoritarian frame of mind and politics are committed to violence and the refusal to support democratic institutions and their principles. This is clear in the Republican Party's decision not to allow their candidate to participate in future presidential debates. As Ruth Ben-Ghiat states, such debates are anathema to the authoritarian mindset. Personality cults posit the leader as a man above all others, and the egalitarian staging and format of debates make them dangerous to his brand. Since authoritarians sustain their power through disinformation, threats, and corruption (including fixing elections), who knows what might be exposed if they submit to spontaneous questioning by a rival or a third party?[18]

Even more shocking was the unqualified praise offered by Trump and his cowardly loyalists to Putin's invasion of Ukraine—a brutal act of aggression that has resulted in massive destruction, bloodshed, a refugee crisis, and heartbreaking suffering for the civilian population. Not only did Trump call Putin "pretty smart" and a "genius," but he also likened the invasion to a real estate deal, stating with no irony intended: "He's taken over a country for $2 worth of sanctions," he said, "taking over a country—really a vast, vast location, a great piece of land with a lot of people— and just walking right in."[19] Such comments are beyond politically reprehensible and morally despicable. This is the language of naked dictatorships and is at the root of fascist ideologies, old and new. Authoritarianism thrives on the language of war and the reality of militarization and is not limited to the Putins of the world.

Warmongering embraces a moral righteousness that rarely reflects on the deep-seated causes of war, including Russia's invasion of Ukraine.[20] Tragic images of the suffering of the Ukrainian people too often appear with little or no critical commentary in the mainstream press. While widespread moral repulsion at the tragedies of the war and Russia's war crimes is understandable, what is not acceptable is the refusal of the mainstream media to reflect on the deeper causes of the war, particularly "the expansion of NATO up to the borders of post-Soviet Russia" and the threat this posed to world peace.[21] As Tariq Ali has argued, the mainstream media's attempts to "dissociate the invasion completely from NATO's aggressive policies over the last few decades" ignore a vital element of both history and contemporary politics.[22] At the same time, there are no excuses for Russia's reckless and brutalizing actions in this war.

Alternatives to violence as a catch-all solution to domestic and global problems run deep in American history and offer a thread that connects demagogues such as Trump, Bolsonaro, and Boris Johnson to the despicable Putin. Violence has become both a source of pleasure and a central element of governance and feeds a dangerous culture of authoritarianism. These are just a few of the many signposts indicating that the revival of fascist conditions that led to January 6 are not only still with us but are becoming normalized and reinvented every day.

Violence in its spectacularized forms tends to produce a shock value that hides the often "slow violence" of everyday life.[23] "Slow violence" is evident in the border violence waged against undocumented immigrants, the scourge of systemic police violence, the homeless deprived of the most basic social provisions, and poor people of color whose culture is equated with criminality and who fill America's prisons.[24] It is also obvious in poor housing conditions, people struggling to put food on the table, and a welfare system in which support payments for the poor tie them to a politics of mere survival and "bare life."[25]

Another element of fascism that has returned with a vengeance is the relationship between fascism and big business.[26] Not only is this evident in the numerous examples of how the financial elite sponsor voter suppression laws, provide millions to push their economic and political interests through lobbying efforts, contribute funds to anti-LGBTQ+ politicians, control the media, and attack government policies that benefit the common good but also in their hoarding of wealth and power.[27]

Necropolitics finds its most powerful expression not only in bombing innocent civilians, or in plans to kidnap and murder dissenting politicians, however horrible such acts are, but also in producing and normalizing forms of massive economic and political inequality that kill and produce massive human suffering.[28] For instance, in a recent report by Oxfam, it is estimated that "inequality is contributing to the death of at least 21,000 people a day, or one person every four seconds."[29] At the same time, "The world's ten richest men more than doubled their fortunes from $700 billion to $1.5 trillion—at a rate of $15,000 per second or $1.3 billion a day—during the first two years of a pandemic that has seen the incomes of 99 percent of humanity fall and over 160 million more people forced into poverty."[30]

Oxfam makes clear that extreme inequality kills, inflicts massive hardships on the vast majority of people on the globe, and "has unleashed this economic violence particularly acutely across racialized, marginalized and gendered lines."[31] Moreover, this greedy financial elite is killing the planet: "the richest 1 percent emit more than twice as much CO_2 as the bottom 50 percent of the world, driving climate change (which contributes) to wildfires, floods, tornadoes, crop failures and hunger."[32] Predatory capitalists such as Elon Musk, Jeff Bezos, and Mark Zuckerberg amass huge profits, contribute to the traffic in death and misery, and pay little in taxes.[33] Oxfam recommends clawing back the tax gains that have been given to the rich and reversing the attack on workers' rights, unions, and the welfare state. Biden promoted legislation, subsequently tanked by Senator Joe Manchin, a West Virginia Democrat, that proposed a tax on the super-rich "with a net worth of $100 million-plus."[34] This was not an insignificant demand, but it said nothing about the relationship between capitalism and fascism, nor does Biden's proposal associate a murderous inequality with a call to end neoliberal capitalism. Moreover, it doesn't even put a dent in stopping runaway wealth inequality.

CHAPTER THREE

The Rebranding of Fascist Politics in the Digital Age

The claims that charges of fascism in America are an overaction appear particularly misplaced and disingenuous, further contributing to the normalization of a rising authoritarianism.[1] This is especially true in the current historical moment of widespread lawlessness, conspiracy theories, a ballooning right-wing propaganda machine, a deadly mix of economic and social inequalities, a growing politics of disposability, and a willingness of large numbers of Republicans to resort to violence to achieve their political goals. What is hard to ignore is that violence and mayhem have become a regular feature of everyday life. Mass shootings happen so often that they are barely reported in the press.[2]

In addition, the culture of politics has turned so toxic that politicians such as Rep. Paul A. Gosar (R-Ariz.) and Rep. Marjorie Taylor Greene have brazenly threatened members of the Democratic Party with violence.[3] Some of their more visible threats include Gosar's anime-style video depiction of him "killing Rep. Alexandria Ocasio-Cortez (D-N.Y.) and swinging swords at Biden."[4] There is also Greene's claim that the only way to get freedom back is "with the price of blood."[5] The latter's call to violence became more specific in a video in which she endorsed "calls to execute FBI agents deemed disloyal to President Donald Trump and to target top Democrats, including 'a bullet to the head' for Speaker Nancy Pelosi."[6]

Such threats are symptomatic of the Republican Party's embrace of lawlessness, violence, nihilism, and the misogyny it brandishes as a badge of honor. Yet, it is important to note that there is more at work here than the nullification of politics and violence as a governing principle; there is also an attempt to destroy truth, empty language of any ethical referents, and disavow any viable view of accountability. Lawlessness and the death of responsibility now find their counterpart, if not legitimating rationale, in a culture of lies and conspiracy theories. As meaning and ethics tip over into the abyss of fascist politics, it becomes easier for fanatical economic, religious, political, and educational fundamentalisms to occupy the centers of power. While economic and market-driven fundamentalisms are hard to miss, the mainstream press says too little about the power of religious fundamentalism in shaping American culture and politics. The collapse of politics into religious fundamentalism is on full display in the actions of former Trump adviser Michael Flynn, who now sees himself as a spokesperson for a fundamentalist religious army while brazenly advocating for a right-wing white Christian takeover of America with his call for "one nation under God and one religion under God."[7] Flynn is symptomatic of the religious war being waged by right-wing radical Christian extremists against both democracy and Christianity. This unholy alliance between Christian extremists and fascism is now a fundamental force in the Republican Party, and its theocratic wing is as dangerous as its menacing group of white supremacists, neo-Nazis, and militia movements.[8] Flynn, in particular, has ties to QAnon and is held up as a hero by a number of far-right fringe organizations and activists, though he is far from the exception among Republican politicians, who in the past would have been considered dangerous threats to democratic values, principles, and institutions.[9]

Religious extremism has a long history in American politics and is resurging once again. It is also important to remember, as Chris Hedges observes, that a major connecting tissue that ties radical extremists to January 6 is what he calls "Christian fascism."[10] Across the United States, religious extremists "are portraying what's happening in America in apocalyptic terms as a grand battle between the forces of good and evil."[11] For instance, the widely popular Pastor Greg Locke, the head of the Global Vision Bible Church in Tennessee, rose to prominence by spreading "the belief that patriotism and love of America are explicitly intertwined with white evangelical Christianity."[12] Locke has a social media following of 4 million and not only retools "Donald Trump's fraudulent claim that the election was stolen as a new holy war," but he also supports burning books such as "Harry Potter" and "Twilight" and has told his followers that "the coronavirus vaccine was made from the tissue of aborted fetuses."[13] Like Michael Flynn, he mixes anti-big government rhetoric and bogus claims about election fraud with hate-filled rhetoric aimed at LGBTQ people and those that oppose the white nationalist evangelical apocalyptic script.

Extremist religious organizations such as Locke's are especially dangerous because they are well funded and rely on an ideological infrastructure that encompasses a series of cultural institutions— systems of communication, universities, and law schools—that have "hermetically sealed millions of Americans" within a regressive, reactionary white supremacist view of the world.[14] Increasingly, the notion of insurrection has become synonymous with the waging of a holy war against migrants, foreigners, and people of color, while escalating the threat of violence and promoting the idea of a fatally wounded and dangerous social order. The historian Geoff Eley captures the diverse elements and conjunctures that hold together a number of groups in this new radicalized, rebranded fascist political formation. He is worth repeating at length. He writes:

> the white supremacism of the overtly fascist groups commingles not only with anger against the Left, but with the wider right-wing contentiousness surrounding cross-border migrancy and the refugee crisis, fear of foreigners, Sinophobia, and generalized Islamophobia. For this broader far-Right militancy, contemporary notations of "race" as cultural belonging, social entitlement, angry intolerance of others, and a narrowly conceived conception of skin and birth-based citizenship supply a main mobilizing animus. These two phenomena increasingly converge: the ideologically self-conscious fascist formations and a broader-based right-wing populism centred around beliefs about race ... The ability of an ever-broadening right-wing coalescence to shift the basic terms of political discourse decisively to the right then becomes troublingly real.[15]

As the conservative columnist David Frum insightfully argues, fascism has emerged in America as a legitimate form of politics, one that welcomes lawless mayhem, a near fascist personality cult, and virulent white supremacy.[16] According to Theda Skocpol, Harvard's renowned sociologist and political scientist, the Republican Party, under Trump's guidance, and backed by billionaires such as the Koch brothers, Sheldon Adelson, Robert Mercer, Blackstone CEO Stephen Schwarzman, and others,[17] has evolved into a radicalized "marriage of convenience between anti-government free-market plutocrats and racially anxious ethno-nationalist activist and voters."[18]

What must be added to this analysis is the role that new forms of media have played in creating the formative culture that fuels the rise of mass demagogery, creating the subjective conditions for the spread of fascist ideology. The digital revolution has created new pedagogical networks that expand and deepen the power of corporate-controlled cultural apparatuses to shape mass consciousness, identities, and politics itself. More specifically, the new social media platforms became powerful propaganda tools and symbols of popular culture for the proponents of fascist politics. One recent example is Trump's use of Twitter to broadcast directly to his base during his presidency. Another crucial example would be the rise of far-right media such as Fox News, Daily Caller, and NewsMaxTV, which have evolved into unabashed propaganda machines.[19]

Other examples would include Facebook and a range of right-wing cable podcasts and alleged news outlets disseminating fascist propaganda. The new digital media platforms have turned toxic in their ability to algorithmically connect fascist groups, provide them with a sense of community, and feed their users conspiracy theories, hate, and bigotry in order "to undermine their ability to comprehend the true source of their alienation."[20]

The offline fascism of the past has rebranded itself, in part, by morphing into an additional register that Thomas Klikauer and Meg Young aptly call "digi-fascism."[21] This online digital fascism focuses on feelings, provides a false sense of an imagined racially cleansed community, rails against minorities threatening white majorities, promotes mass fear, and offers the opportunity for everyone to vent their views and anger without any sense of accountability. Its aim is to mainstream and normalize fascist politics. In doing so, it floods the internet and multiple social media forums with the notion that white people are losing their freedoms, uses anonymity as a tool for individuals to vent their bigotry, threatens the lives of those considered evil enemies, and relies on online conversations to attack "an alien culture determined by the left, feminists, and the state."[22] It also diverts attention away from the brutalizing failures of neoliberalism. In short, "Digi-fascism" is a full-fledged war machine battling against language, values, ideas, and social relations that highlight and deepen the promise of a radical democracy.

What is clear is that digital media has radically changed the landscape of political culture and the realm of the social, sometimes with dangerous results. As Jonathan K. Crary observes, instead of using the vast resources afforded by history, too many people "voluntarily confine themselves in the desiccated digital closets devised by a handful of sociocidal corporations. Pathways to a different world will not be found by internet search engines."[23] What is clear is that not only do social media platforms provide an echo chamber for spreading hate, but under the aegis of neoliberalism they also individualize and privatize politics. Digital media platforms and the internet are not simply new technologies expanding the pedagogical and informational reach of cultural apparatuses, but they are new "machin[eries] of regulation, introducing previously unknown effects of subjection and supervision."[24] Digital fascism is another arena in which the forces of counter-revolution are now waging a war against modernity and those who refuse to live in the shadows of authoritarianism.

For too many people who are willing to give up any sense of critical understanding and agency, the new media substitute emotional stimulation, comfort, and a false sense of community. Protest can now take place from the comfort of one's bedroom rather than in the streets or other social sites. This individualization of politics under global capitalism is one of the major threats to any viable notion of resistance. The habits of solidarity, convictions, and compassion easily drop away as cult figures offer shelter in a storm of anger and confusion, making it all the more possible to embrace the demagogue who presents "himself as the single source of truth."[25]

Under the influence of Trump, image-based politics set the stage for accelerating a politics of fearmongering and the normalization of violence as an article of faith for consolidating power. This is especially true of Fox News's impact on politics, which Steve Schmidt, a former White House adviser to George W. Bush, calls the work of a "death Machine."[26] Barton Gellman is relevant here, given his comments on the vast propaganda army and disinformation campaign that has been key to the pedagogical influence exercised by Trump while in the White House and since leaving it. He writes.

> These forces exert power and influence through relentless disinformation, which continues to turn Americans against Americans. According to the Survey Center on American Life, 36 percent of Americans—almost 100 million adults across the political spectrum—agree that "the traditional American way of life is disappearing so fast that we may have to use force to save it." The *Washington Post* recently reported that roughly 40 percent of Republicans believe that violent action against the government is sometimes justified.[27]

It is impossible to separate the breakdown of civic culture, the collapse of language, and a rise in insurrectionist violence in the United States from the plague of neoliberal capitalism. Under a neoliberal regime of privatized utopias, hyper-individualism, and ego-centered values, humans are immersed in a culture of immediacy, capitalist frenzy, and self-absorption, removed from relations of shared trust and mutual dependency.[28] Self-interest now defines the essence of human behavior, pitting the individual against society. A neoliberal market-driven society has given rise to a culture of precarity, uncertainty, and danger that numbs many people just as it wipes out the creative faculties of imagination, memory, and critical thought. Rather than live in a historical period that awakens the critical faculties, Americans now occupy a social order that freezes and numbs the capacity for informed judgment. Turning away from the collapse of reason, justice, and democracy appears to have become habitual for most Trump supporters. A culture of lies, dishonesty, historical amnesia, distrust, and immorality now fuels an all-consuming politics and machinery of manufactured ignorance. As language has become weaponized, it has been emptied of meaning, reduced to a weapon one would anticipate in a bar brawl. Being stupid in America has become a central principle of politics, the digital landscape, and the GOP view of education.

One might add that when ignorance provides a powerful foundation for supporting authoritarian politicians such as Trump, manufactured thoughtlessness aligns itself on the side of stupidity, criminality, violence, and social death—enfolded by an apocalyptic drive for ruthless power. James Baldwin captured the spirit of moral abandonment and the normalization of violence underlying the merging of ignorance and power when he wrote: "It is certain, in any case, that ignorance, allied with power, is the most ferocious enemy justice can have."[29]

As democracy is increasingly viewed with contempt by large segments of the public, the moral mechanisms of language, meaning, and morality collapse. What emerges is an ethically abysmal collapse of civic consciousness that takes over diverse modes of communication and exchange—a singular register of the rise of a fascist politics. Surely, this is obvious today as all vestiges of the social contract, social responsibility, and modes of solidarity that get people to work together give way to a form of social Darwinism that promotes ruthless forms of competition, privatization, cruelty, war, modes of hyper-masculinity, and a disdain for those considered weak, dependent, alien, or economically unproductive.

A politics of rage, resentment, and illegal legality now translate into policy, as lawmakers in forty-one states do everything possible to block people of color from voting while expanding efforts to undermine free and fair elections. Rules are now passed at the local level to make it easier not only to reject the votes of certain citizens but also to determine "how votes are counted," thus controlling the election process.[30] The war against women's reproductive rights is emerging with hurricane force, as evidenced by the fact that "22 states have abortions bans on their books," now legitmated by the Supreme Court.[31] In addition, lies and conspiracy theories dominate right-wing social media platforms, enhancing their ability "to organize and energize the backlash to democratic movements."[32] Jonathan Haidt rightly captures the role of the powerful right-wing media in producing America's descent into a culture of stupidity. He writes:

> The stupidity on the right is most visible in the many conspiracy theories spreading across right-wing media and now into Congress. "Pizzagate," QAnon, the belief that vaccines contain microchips, the conviction that Donald Trump won reelection— it's hard to imagine any of these ideas or belief systems reaching the levels that they have without Facebook, Twitter and other media platforms.[33]

There is more at work here than an existential crisis nipping at fundamental democratic values; there are a series of insurrections being continually reproduced in the spirit of a longstanding counter-revolution that was unleashed in the 1970s in order to curb the various struggles over democracy. The *New York Times* editorial board captures the spirit of this threat and its recurring actions in its claim "that every day is Jan. 6 now." According to the board, It is regular citizens who threaten election officials and other public servants ... who vow to murder politicians who dare to vote their conscience. It is Republican lawmakers scrambling to make it harder for people to vote and easier to subvert their will if they do. It is Donald Trump who continues to stoke the flames of conflict with his rampant lies and limitless resentments and whose twisted version of reality still dominates one of the nation's two major political parties ... In short, the Republic faces an existential threat from a movement that is openly contemptuous of democracy and has shown that it is willing to use violence to achieve its ends.[34] Trump has even suggested that if he is convicted by any one of a number of ongoing criminal investigations, including the charge of mishandling classified documents, "there would be problems in this country the likes of which we've never see before." This is more than dangerous rhetoric, it is an incitement to his narrowing base of supporters to commit violence as an affirmation of unbridled and lawless loyalty on his behalf.

The forces of counter-revolution present a clear and present danger to the American public. Violence-prone reactionaries and dangerous extremists now control the Republican Party and will stop at nothing to secure power. The United States faces more than an existential crisis. It faces the loss of its withered democracy, freedom, justice, and civil rights with the rise of a nascent and deadly strain of rebranded fascism. As I have said many times, the need for mass political resistance is no longer an option, it is a necessity.

CHAPTER FOUR

The Threat of Remembering

Insurrectional politics and its broader impetus, the force of counter-revolution, cannot be understood by isolating and focusing on the events of January 6. Narrowing the debate about the attack on democracy to the assault on the Capitol creates the conditions for cynicism, apocalyptic despair, and a politics that sabotages itself by virtue of its narrow focus.[1] Moreover, by isolating the event, history vanishes and with it the ability to learn from the past in ways that allow us to further understand the longstanding forces and patterns that work to dissolve the line between democracy and authoritarianism. In the current historical moment, historical amnesia has become normalized and weaponized as a tool of authoritarianism.

The current right-wing attack on history is a form of intellectual violence—a kind of silencing pandemic—that freezes history in an ideological straitjacket, stripping its record of courage, violence, calamity, and change. As Philip Roth stated in *American Pastoral*, "history is reduced to an undetonated past."[2] Remembrance no longer functions as an activity of interrogation, criticism, and renewal dedicated to the promise of freedom;[3] on the contrary, it now functions as an "organized structure of misrecognition."[4] What is under attack by conservative forces is what Toni Morrison described in *Beloved* as "rememory"—a way of thinking memory afresh. As Gabrielle Bellot observes, this takes place in spite of the fact that:

The terrors of the past still live in the present. [As can be seen] in an age when Republicans in Texas and Idaho, among other states have approved legislation prescribing how current events are taught in the classroom severely curtailing discussions of Black American history, and when it is all too common for conservatives to dismiss the existence of systemic racism or the relevance of historical acts of anti-Black violence.[5]

Memory has become a site of repression. Its underlying project is creating a history without an individual and collective democratic subject. Systemic violence, racial injustice, and political corruption have now disappeared from history. History is now frozen in the rigid politics of exclusion. The Republican Party and its political supporters are doing everything they can to make sure that Americans are ignorant of their history. Their goal is to shed the weight of the past, which they consider dangerous. Matters dealing with genocide against Native Americans, the horrors of slavery, Jim Crow, attacks on undocumented immigrants, and a range of other violent moments in American history dissolve into the abyss of censorship. Hence, the attack on resistance movements such as the Civil Rights movement, the Black Lives Matter movement, and movements in defense of LGBTQ+ people. These movements— along with the books, films, and other cultural productions that chart their histories and messages, most notoriously knowledge about slavery, reconstruction, and anti-racist movements—are now portrayed as subversive, and their literature is increasingly banned from schools, libraries, and other public spaces.

As Sasha Abramsky points out, right-wing donors and foundations along with reactionary groups such as Parents Defending Education, Moms for Liberty, Fight for Schools, and Parents Against Critical Theory, have been enormously influential in getting "local officials, legislators and governors in 36 states to either adopt or legislate against the teaching of critical race theory."[6] In this instance, the right-wing censors create convenient fictions under the name of parental responsibility and "comfortable knowledge" in order to disguise and sweep aside troubling knowledge along with questions of race, violence, and economic injustice. At work here is a form of historical repression mediated through disimagination machines that claim to liberate history from the past by denying it. It gets worse.

In a sign of further efforts by Republican politicians to eliminate dissent, unpopular ideas, and tenure, Lt. Gov. Dan Patrick of Texas stated that he wants tenure to be eliminated "for all newly hired faculty members at the state's public universities [and colleges as well as] revoke the tenure of those who teach critical race theory."[7] He offers no evidence in support of this policy, except to denounce, through social media, critical-minded faculty as "looney Marxist ... professors [who] poison the minds of young students with Critical Race Theory."[8] Under the leadership of the African American Policy Forum, a progressive think tank, a number of colleges and universities have passed a resolution designed to protect academic freedom and tenure, and permit the discussion of race and justice issues in the classroom.[9] Increasingly, such groups are also under attack.

According to the self-appointed guardians of "patriotic education," educators who question history or teach controversial issues are now viewed as subversives—a political position not unlike that pushed by the notorious Joseph McCarthy in the 1950s. The new McCarthyism is alive and well in the United States. This type of anti-communism and politically inspired censorship represents an old American political tradition that has taken on a new form. In doing so, it has been re-energized with a language that must be properly understood if it is to be critically interrogated and challenged. For instance, Cameron Joseph reports in *Vice* that GOP Maryland AG hopeful Michael Peroutka "believes public education is a communist plot, abortion and gay marriage violate God's law, and that separation of church and state is a 'great lie'." Peroutka believes that public education should not exist in the United States.

In light of such attacks, it is not enough for progressive educators and others to argue that critical race theory is under attack by right-wing extremists, though this issue is not to be taken lightly. What is in jeopardy is a more serious threat. What I am referring to here is an attempt by the far-right to deny education's critical function by turning critical ideas to ashes. Education is no longer viewed as the practice of freedom and is now attacked by the right-wing propaganda machine as part of a broader effort to destabilize democracy, or what is left of it. Simi Cho, the head of the African American Policy Forum, is right in naming the new McCarthyism and insisting that educators draw from the lessons of history to fight it. She writes:

> The new McCarthyism is not unlike the old McCarthyism, where you just blend something with ad hominem, and freeze the conversation by putting it into this negative category you hope people won't touch. I think by engaging history—what happened

then, what was wrong with it and what we don't want to repeat—those are exactly the sort of lessons we are undertaking with CRT. We look at the problems, the mistakes we've made in the past as a country in terms of structural subordination, unfairness and the ways in which even in an allegedly colorblind society with civil rights laws we are still reproducing rampant, visible and durable inequalities. And if we want to change that, we have to get to the essence of the analysis.[10]

Rather than learn from history by engaging in its complexity, including its horrors, failures, and criminal behavior, right-wing politicians and pundits act as if it didn't exist and when it does, they want to eliminate it from the historical record. No society can ignore the ups and downs of its own history. Any viable social order must be self-reflective about its history in order to move beyond its worst elements. As the journalist Jon Allsop observes, a democratic society cannot be silent about its past and must "be able to challenge its shibboleths [as] an act of self-confidence, not the erosion thereof."[11] The blatant right-wing attempt at erasing the history of slavery and Jim Crow from public education is about more than censorship; it is also about erasing Black and Brown bodies as subjects of history. This is a politics in which certain agents and notions of critical agency disappear. So-called patriotic education, advocated by right-wing politicians, limits identity, subjectivity, and agency to white students, while perpetuating a pedagogy of objectification and ignorance for everyone else.

What is often missed by those who oppose anti-racist educational practices is how crucial they are in educating all students in recognizing and fighting white supremacist forms of ideology, especially at a time when the vast majority of domestic terror attacks are produced by white supremacist extremists. Imram X. Kendi is right in arguing that anti-racist education protects young people against the threat of fasicst ideology and white supremacy in its various forms. He writes:

> But how can white kids–or any kids–guard against this threat if they can't recognize it? How can kids repel ideas of hierarchy if they haven't been taught ideas of equality? How can kids distinguish right from wrong if they haven't been shown what's right and wrong? Recognizing that 'an increasing number of

U.S. teens are getting 'radicalized' online by White supremacists or other extremist groups, an article published by the National Education Association concluded: 'The best place to prevent that radicalization is U.S. classrooms.'[12]

The Republican Party's whitewashing of history and embrace of violence as a political tool takes place through a campaign of misinformation and manufactured ignorance, reproduced and reinforced by Republicans in Congress, right-wing governors and legislators, and their allies in the media. Such efforts are not unrelated to the rewriting of history that took place in Nazi Germany, which also engaged in producing a racially cleansed account of history followed by inconceivable acts of state violence. This authoritarian ghost of ideological repression has returned with a vengeance in the current moment and enables Republican politicians and their followers to revel in historical amnesia, political purity, the whitening of collective identity, and a willingness to wage violence against those who disagree with them, including health workers and policymakers trying to save lives amid the pandemic crisis.

This type of moral nihilism was on full display when the hugely popular Fox News host Tucker Carlson, in an egregious and malicious appropriation of Nazi history, compared Biden's vaccine mandates to Nazi medical practices. This act of historical dishonesty was repeated by Fox News contributor Laura Logan, who likened Dr. Anthony Fauci, Joe Biden's chief medical adviser, to Josef Mengele, the Nazi doctor who was known as the "Angel of Death" for experimenting on Jews in the concentration camps.[13] The use of Nazi Germany as a referent to critique Dr. Fauci, stated without a hint of irony, given that such charges are being made by advocates of white nationalism, white supremacist replacement theory, and the politics of ethnic and racial cleansing, reeks of an unfathomable disingenuousness and moral turpitude. This is the discourse of totalitarians, where words mean whatever they say they mean and in doing so echo how language was maligned in similar ways in the Third Reich.

In the past, these raucous disciples of white supremacy and fascist politics would have "disappeare[d] in a cloud of banality," to borrow a phrase from Hannah Arendt,[14] but today they are celebrated for oozing contempt for democracy, along with utter hatred for those populations they consider superfluous and unworthy of a place in a public sphere defined exclusively for supporters of white nationalism and white evangelical Christianity.

Far-right propagandistic efforts to induce a climate of fear along with a moral and political coma are meant to turn reality on its head, all of which are part of the Republican Party's dangerous efforts to produce a public consciousness trapped in the fog of historical amnesia and manufactured ignorance. The current assortment of Republican zombies are not merely reactionaries for a new age. On the contrary, to paraphrase Raoul Vaneigem, they are people who have corpses in their mouths.[15]

This assault on historical consciousness, reason, and truth is utterly political, given its attacks on critical thinking and its relentless banning of books in schools and libraries. Its goal, among other things, is to prevent open discussions about the history of racism, authoritarianism, and fascism and its relevance to the present. Focusing on the neo-fascistic politics of the Republican Party, Anthony DiMaggio rightly notes

> [I]f we can't have an open, clear, critical discussion about the problem of rising fascism, then people can't recognize the severity of threat. If we don't come to terms with how dangerous this is, then it can just happen and then people don't realize it until it's too late. We need to have a mass movement where people recognize in advance the danger and we work to roll it back.[16]

This right-wing attack on all vestiges of critical education refuses to address the fundamental question of what obligations education has in a democracy. It also avoids a critical rethinking of how knowledge, values, desire, and social relations are implicated in power, as well as questioning the foundations provided for being reflective about oneself, others, and the larger world. In doing so, it undermines the ability of students to learn about community, cooperation, care for the other, the radical imagination, democratic visions, and a commitment to egalitarian justice. This amounts to a pedagogy of repression that promotes a crusade against informed judgments, ensures the waning of political life, supports a withdrawal into private preoccupations, and undermines an attentiveness to the ways in which the absence of critical forms of education breed monsters. I will return to this theme later in the book.

CHAPTER FIVE

Counter-Revolutionary Politics

Exposing fascist politics in the United States is especially critical given that long-repressed echoes of a fascist past can be found in a number of ideas and growing beliefs among Republicans. Forty percent of Republicans, to be exact, believe that violent actions are justified "to achieve political goals" or "resort to violence to save our country."[1] The propagandistic forces promoting public support for political violence have precedents in the vast use of radio, films, theatrical rallies, and right-wing cultural politics to legitimate "fake news," and state violence under Hitler's rule.[2] Hitler's use of the "big lie" and the Nazi's use of diverse forms of propaganda to spread misinformation seem all too familiar today in the aftermath of the Trump presidency.[3] Historian Timothy Snyder writes that fascism " ... begins with a total devotion to persuasive technique, passes through the creation of a pure myth, and ends with the speaker leading his country on a chase for fake phantoms that ends over real graves. In Mein *Kampf*, Hitler wrote that propaganda 'must confine itself to a few points and repeat them over and over.'"[4] This was a propagandistic pedagogical practice that produced a war culture whose goals and tactics have been powerfully revived in different forms in the era of Trumpism. With the merging of gangster capitalism and Trumpism, violence has become promiscuous, visceral, and worn like a badge of honor.

Racism is deeply embedded in the modern Republican Party. This is evident in their passing of voter suppression bills; attempts to subvert election counts; use of racist iconography at many of their rallies; waging an assault on the history of slavery and racism in school curricula; enacting racist attacks on undocumented immigrants, Muslims, and poor Blacks in urban cities; producing racist criticisms of the 1619 Project; and abject display of undying loyalty to Trump, whose racism is well-documented, to mention just a few issues.[5] Under the Trump regime, the "Southern Strategy," embraced by an older Republican Party, morphed into an outright acceptance of white supremacist rhetoric and policies. Among the current Republican base, 57 percent of Republicans believe whites face more discrimination than Blacks,[6] and 46 percent view giving "greater attention to the history of slavery ... negatively."[7] The GOP is over 83 percent white, and its leadership, as Juan Cole states, represents "the white people's party" and is on "the wrong side of history."[8]

The normalization of white hegemony, the collapse of scientific standards, the growing violence saturating everyday life, and the ongoing machinery of a market-driven financial fundamentalism have created a deep sense of cynicism and doom among a wide-ranging cross-section of Americans as well as among intellectuals, pundits, and members of the chattering class.[9] Trapped in their own political and ideological insularity, they largely ignore economic, cultural, and social conditions, as well as historical continuities, which have given rise to the current and dangerous challenges threatening democracy. Consequently, historical memory evaporates, and the past no longer connects with the present. Significant connections between a violent and genocidal past in both the United States and Europe drop out of consideration as the forces of right-wing authoritarianism at all levels of society, especially those involved in the insurrectionist movement, get stronger, more aggressive, and more dangerous.[10]

As more information was revealed in Congressional hearings, it became clear that the assault on the Capitol was far from simply a spontaneous event triggered by incendiary comments by Trump and his associates, who falsely claimed the 2020 election had been stolen—a tactic that made the ensuing violence all the more plausible. On the contrary, the attempt to prevent the peaceful transfer of power and violate constitutional law had been planned at the highest levels of the Trump administration.[11] Support came not only from a number of high-level politicians but also from Gini Thomas, the wife of Supreme Court Justice Clarence Thomas, whose text messages made clear that the drive to overturn the election of Joe Biden went to the highest reaches of government.[12] As constitutional lawyer Laurence H. Tribe observed, "the House Committee ... uncovered evidence of a conspiracy broader, more far-reaching and better organized than was initially thought."[13] But there is more to this act of lawlessness than a conspiracy to prevent a peaceful transition of power and install a minority party to run the country, however illegal. There are also resonances of a long-fermenting counter-revolution that since the 1970s has merged the interests of economic conservatives, a ruling plutocracy, Christian evangelicals, and white supremacists who have "been openly promoting racial hatred and white supremacy for electoral advantage since passage of the civil rights Act in 1964."[14]

As I have mentioned earlier, the January 6 assault cannot be separated from the counter-revolution waged by conservatives in the 1970s against the democratizing movements that erupted in the 1960s. As the "once hopeful dreams of the sixties" receded, the nightmare of neoliberal capitalism emerged.[15] The most significant economic expression of this neoliberal political counter-revolution gained prominence with Reagan's view that government was the problem, not the solution.[16] In this view, markets are given unfettered power and government is reduced to nothing more than a hindrance to the workings of neoliberal capitalism or even worse, their only role is to aid the political and financial interests of gangster capitalism. The economist and noble prize winner Milton Friedman's blunt statement that "the world runs on individuals pursuing their separate ways" became over time a matter of commonsense.[17]

This was a view that brought into high relief the scourge of neoliberalism and its attempt to dismantle the welfare state, pathologize social provisions, and make structural relations of racial and class power disappear, all the while setting the stage for the financial elite to amass unprecedented amounts of wealth and power.[18] The market became a template for all of society and was "entrusted with the tasks most societies reserve almost exclusively for government: health care, pensions, low-income housing, education, social services and incarceration."[19] The welfare state and social safety nets were reduced to outdated burdens, viewed by Republicans and some Democrats, such as President Bill Clinton, as a problem rather than a solution. In addition, attacks on the welfare state coincided with the claim that self-interest and individual choice were the only reliable forces shaping human agency, a claim perfect for reducing citizenship to the obligations of consumption and nothing more.

Before the 1980 election of Ronald Reagan, the ideological foundation of the counter-revolution was defined in the 1970s by the Powell Memo and later the Trilateral Commission, both of which lauded capitalism and disdained movements for social change and racial justice as symptomatic of an "an excess of democracy."[20] Needless to say, the Democratic Party also played a significant role in the emergence of neoliberalism in the United States. Jeffrey St. Claire sums it up well. He writes:

> Of course, the neoliberal transformation of the Democratic Party has been a long-time coming. It began under Jimmy Carter and reached its apotheosis under Bill Clinton, who boldly declared the end to the era of "Big Government" and began the systematic dismantling of the FDR/LBJ welfare state from the inside, including the welfare system itself.[21]

Under the Trump administration, neoliberalism emerged on steroids, with huge tax cuts for the rich, a further dismantling of environmental and corporate regulations, and an entrepreneurial mindset that gave new meaning to greed and political corruption. At the same time, a different element of the counter-revolution emerged that I have labeled neoliberal fascism.[22] Neoliberal fascism is a direct outgrowth of the failure of market-based capitalism to contain intolerable levels of economic inequality and defend the myth of meritocracy. In its attempt to avoid a legitimacy crisis in the past, the ruling class in America responded to social problems with mass incarceration, but that policy ran its course as the policy was increasingly exposed as a central element of systemic racism. Gangster capitalism increasingly revealed itself through the workings of a state that could no longer legitimate its failures by blaming poor Blacks and an impoverished working class for not climbing the ladder of social mobility. While this argument resembled the older post-racial argument that Blacks were marked by cultural deficiencies, it integrated this notion into a much more repugnant notion of disposability—the notion that Blacks were not deserving of occupying any space in the public sphere.

Neoliberalism's appeal to meritocracy gave way to the quick fix of white supremacy and a growing authoritarianism. Turning to the discourse of white nationalism, racial bigotry, and a war on youth, neoliberal fascism now uses its ideological weapons to create a broad swath of enemies, including poor people of color, undocumented immigrants, transgender youth, women seeking reproductive rights, and young people, the latter demonized and dehumanized for believing in the right to a quality education and gender justice. Neoliberal fascism is a political and economic ideology that attacks the welfare state and its principal notion that "the state can and should be the guardian of the people's interest";[23] it also incorporates a fascist politics rooted in a discourse of white supremacy and a politics of exclusion. In this new historical context, neoliberalism did not abandon the elements of the Reagan counter-revolution but provided a rationale and diversion for the increasing failure of free-market fundamentalism by attacking the responsibility of the federal government in solving social problems. At the same time, it attempts to cover up "what we tend to think of as racial inequality from political economy."[24] Given these concerns, it is crucial to stress another condition promoting an ongoing counter-revolution in the United States.

In this instance, I am referring to the counter-revolution waged around identity, bruised agency, and manufactured stupidity, rooted in the radical integration of culture, power, and technology. Today this political formation is far more dangerous than any others in the last fifty years. Central to this political formation is the refashioning of identity through the all-encompassing discourse of consumerism, replacement theory, a weakening of the bonds of solidarity and mutual care, a growing movement for the establishment of Christianity as a state religion, a depoliticizing and elevated emphasis on the inner self, and the anti-structural language of the therapeutic.[25] The ideological bedrock of this counter-revolution is largely legitimated and powerfully amplified through a toxic profit-seeking social media that has done enormous damage to democracy over the last few years, especially with its embrace of a "militantly racialized nationalism" that demonized "refugees, asylum-seekers, migrants ... and people of color."[26]

The Republican Party's call to lawlessness and its increasing appeal to violence as a tool of political opportunism reached fever pitch during the Trump administration. Trump's contempt for democracy and bitter revenge fantasies have been relentlessly propagated as part of a well-funded propaganda machine that purposely spreads conspiracy theories and false information, dissolves the border between truth and falsehoods, and amplifies the appeal to white nationalism.[27] Legal illegalities are on the rise, as conservative courts legitimate restrictive voting rights, accelerate the assault on women's reproductive rights by overturning Roe vs. Wade., and justify secret donor contributions to charities—opening the door for the influx of more "'anonymous' money into the political system."[28] In the post-Trump era, the role of dark money has exploded in American politics. A trend that Jane Mayer, as part of her investigation of right-wing funding groups, identifies as a politics that produces what she calls the rise of "the slime machine."[29] This is also a politics that breathes new life into rule by the financial elite, a culture of cruelty, and a white supremacist ideology that echoes a dangerous and foreboding past.

PART TWO

Social Media and the Fascist Threat

CHAPTER SIX

Social Media as a Disimagination War Machine

Right-wing corporate media and its pseudo-thinkers are essential components of a cultural war machine. This war machine fuels a media ecosystem of fear, deception, and violence and is one of the underlying forces fomenting a vast array of insurrections in America. The latter was evident not only in the January 6 assault on the Capitol but also in the truck convoy protests or "Freedom Convoy" insurrection that became a driving force in spreading counter-revolutionary movements around the globe. In both instances, language was armed, steeped in an affirmation of violence, and dedicated to undoing democratic values and the institutions that embrace them, all the while falsely making appeals to "freedom." Moreover, in this atmosphere of corruption, the wall collapses between governance and right-wing media. Not only did right-wing digital and mainstream media support both reactionary movements, but they also played a significant role in spreading their ideology of hate globally. They were aided, of course, by a coterie of right-wing politicians such as Josh Harley and Ted Cruz along with a range of Fox News pundits. One striking example related to the January 6 insurrection was a report in *The Washington Post*, which stated that Sean Hannity and "Judge" Jeanine Pirro, both of whom host prime-time Fox News shows, served "as a cable cabinet of unofficial advisers" in order to overturn the Biden election and spread fabrications, conspiracy theories, and a disdain for evidence and facts.[1]

Subsequently, "the big steal", among other red flags, becomes more than a lie; it becomes the architectural machinery of an ideological ecosystem that works relentlessly to destroy truth as a foundational element of democracy. Cartoon TV hosts and podcast celebrities such as Joe Rogan emerge as the bearers of misinformation, using the power of social media to spread misrepresentations that fuel a culture wedded to violence and seditious insurrectionary acts. Cultural war machines, including infotainment media, are now replete with their own groomed and slavishly loyal mercenaries who operate in the service of organized irresponsibility, hate, and necropolitics. Cultural power now corrupts, spreads ignorance and hate, and depoliticizes large elements of the public while producing a failed state.

This echo chamber of propaganda also includes right-wing extremists and Trump allies such as former New York mayor Rudy Giuliani, who "encouraged domestic terrorist behavior aimed at preventing Congress from certifying the outcome of the 2020 presidential election," and former White House chief strategist Steve Bannon, who has publicly called for the beheading of Dr. Anthony Fauci, director of National Institute of Allergy and Infectious Diseases, and Christopher Wray, head of the Federal Bureau of Investigation.[2] Bannon is considered a hero among many well-known white supremacists, including former Ku Klux Klan leader David Duke and Peter Brimelow, the head of the racist, white nationalist site VDare.[3] Bannon joins a number of Republicans who want to militarize politics and society as part of a larger project in which "civil society organizes itself for the production of violence."[4] Rather than being viewed as deranged, corrupt political actors, these Republicans are now treated as heroes in the conservative media.

As the debate about the insurrection moved between spectacle, with its focus on cartoonish characters dressed like Abraham Lincoln, Lady Liberty, and of course, the "Q-Anon Shaman" guy, on the one hand, and the immediate vandalism and transgressive actions of the insurrectionist mob, on the other, the historical and contemporary roots of the insurrection were initially downplayed and, in some cases, vanished from the mainstream media. The exceptions consisted of a few journalists and historians of Europe who connected the insurrection's elements of a sordid fascist past to the Republican Party's appropriation of some of its white supremacist ideological baggage. The tragedy here is that the boundary between politics and criminality dissolved. Moreover, the mobilizing passions of a fascist past in an updated spectacularized form became a driving force in American politics. Fortunately, as James Risen observed, in an "attention-deficit America," the House Select Committee investigating the January 6 attack "provided a gut-punch reminder of just how violent and dangerous the insurrection was [and] how much of a threat to American democracy remains today from the right-wing furies unleashed by Trump."[5]

It is important to note that despite the Trump regime's threat to democracy and its increasingly boldfaced fascist politics, the mainstream media for too long underplayed the corruption and anti-democratic values and policies at work within it, giving it ample time to consolidate its authoritarian forces away from the public view.[6] Initially, the sacking of the Capitol by domestic terrorists was rarely analyzed as a planned and coordinated attack by Trump and a high-level number of politicians and right-wing individuals. It is worth repeating that what was eventually recognized both at home and abroad was not only that the violent attack on the Capitol was planned and coordinated by a number of high-ranking Republican Party operatives, but it also constituted a major political and constitutional crisis in the making. But recognition of the seriousness of the insurrection did not lead to a more profound understanding of its underlying historical, political, and economic causes. The sheer boldness, violence, and danger the assault presented created a political crisis that was not matched by a crisis of ideas or a crisis of historical reckoning. That is, a dearth of attention was given to the possibility that something deeper was at issue. In a time of manufactured ignorance, cultural politics succumbs to a culture of immediacy, militarism, and the scourge of presentism. Coverage of the brutal Russian invasion of Ukraine exemplifies both the decline of critical commentary and the death of civic culture.

With the war in Ukraine raging, more nuanced analyses, along with dissent, disappear in the suffocating discourses of hyper-nationalism and the growing bonfire of militarism fueled by what Indian essayist and novelist Pankaj Mishra calls "an infotainment media [that] works up citizens into a state of paranoid patriotism."[7] The military-industrial-intellectual-academic complex has reasserted itself in the face of Russia's violation of international law, accelerating the prospect of, if not welcoming, another looming

Cold War, aided greatly by media apparatuses that bask in the comfort of moral certainty and patriotic inanity. In this atmosphere of hyper-war culture, military victories become synonymous with moral victories, as language becomes weaponized and matters of ethics no longer inform the urgent call for peace.

In the face of the vicious Russian invasion, the concept of insurrection is amplified and put into service as a call for resistance against Russian savagery. The response to savagery wins out over ways to search for a just peace, prioritize diplomacy, and eliminate conditions that could result in a nuclear war. Talk of war not peace dominates the media platforms. Such talk also fuels a global arms industry, oil and gas monopolies, and the weaponization of language itself.[8] Insurrection as a tool of unchecked nationalism and patriotism drives the mainstream and right-wing disimagination machines. Both fuel global war fever through different degrees of misrepresentation and create what intellectual historian Jackson Lears calls "an atmosphere poisoned by militarist rants."[9] He goes further in his critique of the US response to the war in Ukraine, writing in the *New York Review of Books*:

> Yet the US has failed to put a cease-fire and a neutral Ukraine at the forefront of its policy agenda there. Quite the contrary: it has dramatically increased the flow of weapons to Ukraine, which had already been deployed for eight years to suppress the separatist uprising in the Donbas. US policy prolongs the war and creates the likelihood of a protracted insurgency after a Russian victory, which seems probable at this writing. Meanwhile, the Biden administration has refused to address Russia's fear of NATO encirclement. Sometimes we must conduct diplomacy with nations whose actions we deplore. How does one negotiate with any potential diplomatic partner while ignoring its security concerns? The answer, of course, is that one does not. Without serious American diplomacy, the Ukraine war, too, may well become endless.[10]

The horrific events in the Ukraine have mobilized a global response against the savage acts of violence inflicted on the Ukrainian people. Yet what is often ignored in the mainstream media is that such massive acts of violence have also taken place in Syria, Afghanistan, Iraq, and Yemen without eliciting comparable condemnations or humanitarian aid from the United States and Europe. Moreover, while public outrage in the United States is warranted in light of the "horrendous crimes by Russian troops against Ukrainian civilians—massacre, murder, and rape, among them," memory fades, and the line between fantasy and historical consciousness disappears, "erasing the brutalizing crimes committed during America's Global War on Terror."[11]

US foreign policy is immersed in blood; torture; the violations of civil rights; abductions; kidnappings; targeted assassinations; illegal black holes; the scorched bodies of members of a wedding party in Yemen killed by a drone attack; and hundreds of women, children, and old men brutally murdered by US soldiers in the Vietnam village of My Lai.

In a war culture, memory fades, violence is elevated to its most visible and mediating force, and logic is reconfigured to feed a totalitarian sensibility. Under such circumstances, as London School of Economics Professor Mary Kaldor has argued, we live at a time in which the relationship between politics and violence is changing. She states: "Rather than politics being pursued through violent means, violence becomes politics. It is not conflict that leads to war but war itself that creates conflict."[12]

Behind this disproportionate response by the international community and its media platforms lies the ghosts of colonialism and the merging of culture with the undercurrents of white supremacy. For example, the general indifference to comparable acts of war and unspeakable violence can be in part explained by the fact that the Ukrainian victims appearing on the mass media are white Europeans. What is not shown are "Black people being refused at border crossings in favor of white Ukrainians, leaving them stuck at borders for days in brutal conditions [or] Black people being pushed off trains."[13] The mainstream media celebrate Poland's welcoming of Ukrainian refugees but are silent about the Polish government boasting of building walls and "creating a 'fortress' to keep out refugees from Syria and Afghanistan."[14]

It is easy for white people in the media to sympathize with people who look just like them. This was made clear when CBS News Senior Correspondent Charlie D'Agata, reporting on the war, stated that it was hard to watch the violence waged against Ukrainians because Ukraine "isn't a place, with all due respect, like Iraq or Afghanistan that has seen conflict raging for decades. This is a relatively civilized, relatively European [country] ... one where you wouldn't expect that or hope that it's going to happen."[15] In this case, "civilized" is code for white. D'Agata simply echoed the obvious normalization of racism, as is clear in a number of comments that appeared in the mainstream press. *The Guardian* offered a summary of just a few, which include the following:

> The BBC interviewed a former deputy prosecutor general of Ukraine, who told the network: 'It's very emotional for me because I see European people with blue eyes and blond hair ... being killed every day.' Rather than question or challenge the comment, the BBC host flatly replied, 'I understand and respect the emotion.' On France's BFM TV, journalist Phillipe Corbé stated this about Ukraine: 'We're not talking here about Syrians fleeing the bombing of the Syrian regime backed by Putin. We're talking about Europeans leaving in cars that look like ours to save their lives ... And writing in the Telegraph, Daniel Hannan explained: 'They seem so like us. That is what makes it so shocking. Ukraine is a European country. Its people watch Netflix and have Instagram accounts, vote in free elections and read uncensored newspapers. War is no longer something visited upon impoverished and remote populations.'[16]

There is more here than a slip of the tongue; there is also the repressed history of white supremacy. As City University of New York Professor Moustafa Bayoumi observes, all of these comments point to a deeply ingrained and "pernicious racism that permeates today's war coverage and seeps into its fabric like a stain that won't go away. The implication is clear: war is a natural state for people of color, while white people naturally gravitate toward peace."[17]

Clearly, in the age of Western colonialism, a larger public is taught to take for granted that justice should weigh largely in favor of people whose skin color is the same as those who have the power to define whose lives count and whose do not. These comments are also emblematic of the propaganda machines that have resurfaced with the blight of racism on their hands, indifferent to the legacy of white exceptionalism with which they are complicit.

Historical amnesia and a prolonged military conflict combine, making it easier to sell war rather than peace, which would demand not only condemnation of Russia but also an exercise in self-scrutiny with a particular focus on the military optic that has been driving

US foreign policy since President Dwight D. Eisenhower warned in the 1950s of the danger of the military-industrial complex.

The Ukrainian war is truly insidious and rouses the deepest sympathies and robust moral outrage, but the calls to punish Russia overlook the equally crucial need to call for peace. In doing so, such actions ignore a crucial history and mode of analysis that make clear that behind this war are longstanding anti-democratic ideologies that have given us massive inequality, disastrous climate change, poverty, racial apartheid, and the increasing threat of nuclear war.

War never escapes the tragedies it produces and is almost always an outgrowth of the dreams of the powerful—which always guaranties a world draped in suffering and death. Peace is difficult in an age when culture is organized around the interrelated discourse of militarism and state violence. War has become the only mirror in which authoritarian societies recognize themselves. Rather than being defined as a crisis, war for authoritarian rulers and the soulless arms industries becomes an opportunity for power and profits, however ill conceived. Peace demands a different assertion of collective identity, a different ethical posture and value system that takes seriously Martin Luther King Jr.'s admonition that human beings must do everything not to "spiral down a militaristic stairway into the hell of nuclear annihilation."[18] Surely, he was correct in adding that "Mankind must put an end to war or war will put an end to mankind."[19] King was right in his call to find a new language to speak of peace, for justice, and of a future that is not blinded by the poison of war. This is not merely a matter of conscience or resistance but survival itself.

CHAPTER SEVEN

Capitalism's Observation Posts and the Politics of Denial

Denial and disappearance are central to the politics of the mainstream media. For instance, the corporate-controlled media largely ignored the growing threat of an updated form of authoritarianism that had been slowly growing in the United States since the election of Ronald Reagan in 1980. The fascist politics at work during reconstruction and the emergence of the civil rights movement took on a new register with the merging of white supremacist ideology and the savage mechanisms of a neoliberal economy, both of which were powerful forces in creating the conditions for the insurrection.[1] The underlying necropolitics driving the surge of right-wing populism and the attack on the Capitol was largely decoupled from neoliberal capitalism and its related institutions of violence. These include white nationalism, massive inequality, the prison-industrial complex, the politics of disposability, unchecked militarization, and persistent racism.[2]

As I mentioned earlier, a range of propagandistic cultural apparatuses was central to producing and legitimating these anti-democratic forces. C. Wright Mills criticized these as "the observation posts, the interpretation centres, the presentation depots" of pedagogical repression.[3] What Mills was referring to and concerned about were dominant machineries of representation and how they worked to normalize a market-driven economy, reproduce consumer identities, and narrate notions of commonsense through a developing web of photocentric, aural, and screen cultures. This is a fundamental issue in the current moment given that Republican outrage over everything that promotes democratic values has been amplified and largely produced as a "TV-worthy performance," without any attempt to address fundamental social and economic issues such as massive inequality, ecological degradation, the collapse of public education, and the power of finance capital.

Fundamental to the right-wing attack on democracy is a counter-revolutionary politics, the aim of which was to elevate white nationalist rule and a politics of disposability. Politics has turned deadly with the rise of an authoritarian narrative, in which, as Mbembe states in a different context, those who do not matter are relegated to "death worlds ... forms of social existence in which vast populations are subjected to conditions of life conferring upon them the status of *living dead*."[4] Surely, this form of necropolitics applies to the US government's treatment of undocumented immigrants, poor people of color, the homeless, the incarcerated, the victims of racist police violence, and the elderly in long-term care facilities—especially in the age of the pandemic.[5]

Violence is never far removed from the politics of denial. The response to the attack by Trump and his loyalists elevated denial to a form of symbolic violence. Republican Party politicians entered the realm of the delusional by denying the seriousness of the attack on the Capitol, claiming it was no more than a nonviolent, peaceful protest waged by "patriotic Americans." Former President Trump publicly stated that the assault amounted to a minor act of trespassing, a "zero threat from the start." He also claimed that the armed insurrectionists were "innocent and peaceful people," unfairly subject to overzealous criminal persecution, and, without a hint of self-reflection, further stated on Fox News that "there was such love at that rally."[6] What he dutifully ignored was that the insurrectionists came armed with baseball bats, tasers, knives, truncheons, bear mace, body armor, firearms, and anything else they could use to attack the police.[7] Trump's egregious lies worked well, with a further act of denial in which he claimed that the real insurrection took place on November 3, the day Biden won the election.[8] Trump has not only repeatedly claimed the attempt to overthrow the government on January 6 was a legitimate expression of protests, but he also stated in an interview with *The Washington Post* on April 7, 2022 that he regretted "not marching to the U.S. Capitol the day his supporters stormed the building."[9]

Even worse, the outright fascist wing of the Republican Party, including Senator Ted Cruz and Representatives Marjorie Taylor Greene and Matt Gaetz—later joined by Fox News commentator Tucker Carlson—detoured quickly into paranoia by claiming the assault was either produced by leftist militants or the FBI. Newt Gingrich topped them all by claiming Nancy Pelosi was responsible for the assault. Gaetz and Greene have become two of the most vocal supporters of the false claim that those arrested for violating the Capitol were political prisoners. It gets worse. Some Georgia Republicans wanted to hold a vigil, a year after the assault on the Capitol, "praying—not just for those killed or hurt during the Jan. 6 riot but also for the 'J6 Prisoners' and 'J6 Patriots' who stormed the building in a futile attempt to keep President Donald Trump in power."[10] One commentator correctly labeled the plan a "homage to treason."[11]

Most of these disillusioned liars would be charged along with Trump and his followers with seditious conspiracy in a sane and just world. Such a charge could easily be expanded to almost the entirety of the Republican congressmen and women who in the hours after the attempted siege "formally disputed the election result," ending any possibility of repudiating the "big lie".[12] Moreover, by refusing any attempt to challenge and call out Trump, they legitimated "the reality of the violence he caused."[13] Furthermore, by refusing to accept Biden's electoral victory, they became complicitous and active participants in intensifying the war on democratic institutions and normalizing a growing culture of violence. Such actions represented a turning point in America's turn toward fascism. Thom Hartmann is right in stating that "There's always been a fringe movement of violent white supremacist vigilantes in America, particularly since the end of the Civil War, but they've never before been embraced by or succeeded in capturing a political party. Today, astonishingly, that's the case in our country."[14]

While it became increasingly clear that democracy was under siege, little was said about something inherent in the unfolding of a savage and ruthless capitalism and its seamless alignment with a fascist politics. Lost here were the workings of a neoliberal regime with its massive inequalities in wealth and private power, its comfortable alliance with structural racism, and a political system driven by money and the concentrated control of the ultra-rich and corrupt financial institutions. This is an economic system with profound malignancies, one that has given rise to pernicious relations of power that have transformed the Republican Party into a force that, as Noam Chomsky states, "is driving organized human society to suicide." He further argues that, however weak democracy is in the United States, it "is intolerable to the GOP wreckers."[15] He writes:

> But even the tattered system that still survives is intolerable to GOP wreckers. Nothing is overlooked in their systematic assault on the fragile structure. Methods extend from "taking hold of the once-overlooked machinery of elections" at the ground level, to passing laws to bar the "wrong people" from voting, to devising a legal framework to establish the principle that Republican legislatures can "legally" determine choice of electors, whatever the irrelevant public many choose.[16]

It is worth repeating that what was overlooked in most accounts of the mob assault was the "slow-motion" fascist-inspired insurrection that had been brewing for years as a counter-revolution. This was a counter-revolution against the calls for democratization that had emerged in the sixties with the affirmation of collective agency, the expansion of political rights for marginalized people of color, and the call for equality and social justice.

Racial hatred is deeply rooted in American history, and it was on full display in the mob-fueled attack on the Capitol. Beneath the overt hatred of democracy, the mob exhibited not only a defense of violence mixed with contempt for universal rights but also a white supremacist vision of who qualifies for citizenship and what it means to be an American. Fueled by a view of distressed agency and victimhood, the insurrectionists and most of Trump's followers support the "big lie" not because it has little regard for evidence, but because it further legitimates the larger narrative that white people are under siege and that whatever rights and privileges are extended to people of color will take place at the expense of white people. This view embodies the fascist notion of never having to say you are sorry for inhabiting the realm of the barbaric. The writer Fintan O'Toole is right in arguing that what drives Trump's mob of followers is the power to say who counts as an American and who does not. He writes:

> the mob's core demand is more fundamental. It wants the power to say who is real and who is not. The phrase that echoed throughout the invasion of the Capitol was "This is our house." It is a double claim of belonging—both "we belong here" and "this belongs to us." It is an assertion of title ... [At work here is the] fusing the idea of an entitlement to privilege—which is being stolen from white Americans by traitors, Blacks, immigrants, and socialists—with the absolute distinction between real and unreal Americans. The concern is not, at heart, that there are bogus votes, but that there are bogus voters, that much of the US is inhabited by people who are, politically speaking, counterfeit citizens.[17]

The Republican Party's embrace of xenophobic nationalism and fascist politics is not only displayed in policies aimed at voter suppression, gerrymandering, and the rewriting of election laws but also in their catering to white fears and the willingness to strike a mortal blow to democracy. The Republicans' war, led by its most extremist elements, on democratic institutions is brutally clear regarding its attempts to impose a minority government and take power away from the American people.

One major scenario imagining the death of democracy centers on the possibility of a bloodless coup conducted not by vigilantes or "rioters with nooses" but "lawyers in fine suits."[18] John Eastman, a Trump lawyer, illustrated one example of this tactic. Eastman put together a document aimed at convincing former Vice President Mike Pence to "throw out the electoral votes of key swing states on the basis that they had competing slates of electors."[19] Needless to say, the plan failed, and the goal of undermining fair elections has now switched from the federal level to undermining election results at the state and local levels.

In a widely read article in *The Atlantic,* Barton Gellman argues that the movement to destroy democracy in the United States will rely primarily on subverting voting rights and other forms of election theft. In this view, the claim of voter fraud, which is exceedingly rare, has morphed into the truly dangerous discourse of election fraud, used by the right to produce many legal illegalities to manipulate the system to overturn the voters' will.[20] With a certain degree of fatalism, George Packer argues that the greatest danger to democracy in the United States comes from a potentially rigged election implemented through widespread laws to enact voter suppression and take control over election results. He writes:

> There is no easy way to stop a major party that's intent on destroying democracy. The demonic energy with which Trump repeats his lies, and Bannon harangues his audience, and Republican politicians around the country try to seize every lever of election machinery—this relentless drive for power by American authoritarians is the major threat that America confronts. The Constitution doesn't have an answer. No help will come from Republican leaders; if Romney and Susan Collins are all that stand between the republic and its foes, we're doomed.[21]

Another scenario is that a slow-motion civil war and counter-revolution might emerge in a system in which millions of Republicans will be convinced by Trump and his ideological apparatchiks to use bloodshed to achieve their political aims. Following this logic, the more extremists elements loyal to Trump will engage in a series of armed insurrections in order to throw the government into chaos, force the imposition of martial law, and segue into a modern-day dictatorship.[22] Accordingly, the idea of a violent insurrection takes on the mantle of a sacred cause fueled by a "relentless drive for power by American authoritarians."[23] What is interesting about this position, strongly argued by Gellman, is that it presents the January 6 assault as a rehearsal for further acts of violence and subversion, reiterating the *New York Times* position that "January 6th is now every day."[24]

CHAPTER EIGHT

Politics as Civil War and the Culture of Violence

George Packer, Barton Gellman, and several other scholars have argued that the threat of insurrection and civil war will not occur based on some states seceding, or as Lincoln Mitchell puts it, "two American armies fighting each other."[1] On the contrary, the prevailing assumption is that insurrections will result from fracturing among different political groups disputing the outcome of stolen elections, especially in 2024. This fracturing is part of the Republican playbook for imposing an authoritarian order on the American people.

Clearly, the Republican Party functions like an insurgency by flaunting lawlessness, using "the threat of violence as a tool of intimidation,"[2] hollowing out democratic institutions, and exhibiting contempt for legality. Zak Cheney-Rice, writing in *New York Magazine*, is on target in stating that not only is the Republican Party obsessed with crime, but it has also become a criminogenic political formation. He writes:

> The Republican Party under Donald Trump is obsessed with crime. In its efforts to overturn the results of the 2020 election, it has cast Democratic victories as illegal and illegitimate. In order to win elections in the future, it has passed a slew of restrictive voting laws on the state level that characterize Democratic votes as fraudulent. And to conjure a climate of fear, it has

depicted Democratic-controlled metropolises as being overrun by murderers and overwhelmed by violence. The GOP wants voters to see crime everywhere—at the ballot box, swallowing cities whole.[3]

The elements of the Republican Party's resuscitated counter-revolutionary strategy are on full display in its relentless expressions of rage against the press, educated elites, and those critical of Republican Party policies. At the same time, it works feverishly to shut down dissent, spread lies, legitimate Trump's lust for revenge, and unabashedly trade in ethnic, religious, racial, and cultural hatreds, "probably the most universal feature of fascism."[4] The spirit of authoritarianism is widely pervasive and is deeply ingrained in America.

Some influential writers such as Fintan O'Toole dismiss all talk regarding a possible civil war, suggesting that such talk distracts from dealing with more concrete issues such as holding those accountable who defy the law. He summarizes this position with a relatively weak comment, in which he states: "The dark fantasy of Armageddon distracts from the more prosaic and obvious necessity to uphold the law and establish political and legal accountability for those who encourage others to defy it. Scary stories about the future are redundant when the task of dealing with the present is so urgent."[5] That may have been correct before Trump's mob smashed up the Capitol, but it is no longer true. The potential for fascist violence among the millions of Americans who support it is far from an empty "dark fantasy," especially since four out of ten Republicans believe violence might be warranted to allow Trump to rule the country.[6]

This right-wing acceptance of mass violence is all the more ominous given that the conditions for a counter-revolution to emerge in America are already in place. This is evident in the current war on reproductive rights, education, regulations designed to control an environmental catastrophe, affordable health care, and any other issue designed to further social justice. What is unique about this war is that it is not only being waged by fringe groups but also by the modern Republican Party. Civil war, in this instance, is not, as I mentioned earlier, a referent for open warfare between two groups but a forecast about the seriousness of the danger facing American democracy. It also points to an altered meaning of politics in which, to paraphrase Carl von Clausewitz, politics has become a continuation of war by other means.[7]

It is worth noting that much of the current discourse regarding the threat of civil war fails to acknowledge that the underlying threat to American democracy comes not only from the increasing recourse to violence on the part of mostly Trump's followers but also because of its prominence as a defining feature of politics. Armed violence and lawlessness now feed each other with the help of massive disimagination machines relentlessly spreading misinformation and disinformation.[8] Violence has become a central feature of a militarized society aided and abetted by the scorched earth tactics of right-wing media platforms that trade in falsifications and the massive erasure of historical memory. It is crucial to remember that the turn toward fascist politics in the United States has a long history rooted deeply in acts of genocide against Native Americans, the scourge of slavery, Jim Crow violence, the erasure of historical memory, and upgraded forms of systemic racism buttressed by a merging of white supremacy, the rise of the punishing state, staggering inequality, unchecked political corruption, and a pervasive culture of fear and insecurity. As history is blindsided by the Republican Party, political and social amnesia rule America, unleashing a dreadful plague of violence on civic life, proving that fascism lives in every culture and that it only takes a spark to ignite it.

In the world of image-based politics, theater replaces any notion of meaningful politics and is "complicit in the perpetuation of violence on a mass scale."[9] This new cultural techno-sphere of violence has become spectacularized, "facilitated by the degradation of language, the proliferation of cultural apparatuses dedicated to misinformation, and ... the expropriation of the senses."[10] This culture of violence does not merely shape the social fabric in the image of savage capitalism; it devastates it.

America has entered a new and more dangerous cold war, waged at home rather than exclusively on the world stage. In the post-Trump era, democracy can no longer defend even its principles, which fade out against the demands of the billionaire class and its global crime syndicate. Class, racial, and gender divisions have become ossified, rendering the social fabric fragmented, fractured, and vulnerable to what Jonathan Crary describes as "more predatory and lethal forms of repression and neglect."[11] In the current historical moment, the catastrophic brutality of authoritarianism embraces violence as a legitimate tool of political power, opportunism, and a vehicle to squelch dissent and terrorize those labeled as enemies because they are either people of color or insufficiently loyal to Trumpism—or oppose the white-Christian reactionary view of women, sexual orientation, and religious extremism. Violence in this instance is not hidden; it is displayed by the Republican Party and the financial elite as both a threat to induce fear and a spectacle to mobilize public emotions. This is a form of lethal violence that is both embraced as a strategy and covered over with lies in order to disavow the consequences, however deadly.

As I mentioned previously, the concept of civil war is about much more than different groups engaging in violence against each other—one group working to defend democracy and the other to destroy it. Limiting civil war to the willingness of people to resort to arms to fight for a political goal overlooks a much broader struggle over how politics is defined, how it is shaped, and what narratives it embraces regarding how the future will be played out. Civil war is now a governing principle of politics rather than its endpoint. In the current era of emerging authoritarianism and unleashed bigotry, the concept of war has taken on a much more capacious meaning, and David Theo Goldberg points to a "politics that has become nothing short of civil war."[12] According to Goldberg,

> politics and war have become indistinguishable ... Civil war is no longer the end of politics but its normalized expression ... This extended sense of civil war is less one segment of society at increasingly dissonant odds with another. It is the society as such at war with itself, an allergic condition of civil society eating at itself from the inside out.[13]

Trump's insurrectionists have every reason to believe that they are not accountable for the violence they have committed and will commit in the future. They do not recognize the seriousness of their ongoing criminal behavior, including the mob assault on January 6, not only because they believe the 2020 presidential election was stolen but also because they no longer believe in the rule of law or the legitimacy of informed judgments and evidence. How else to explain the ongoing attacks on the Constitution, the shredding of shared values, and the endless lies and conspiracy theories that undermine truth, justice, and the law itself.

The Republican Party's appeal to lawlessness and violence took a dangerous turn at a comeback Trump rally in Conroe, Texas in January 2022. Trump declared that if he wins the election in 2024, he will pardon the January 6 insurrectionists, stating, "If I run and I win, we will treat those people from Jan. 6 fairly," adding, "And if it requires pardons, we will give them pardons, because they are being treated so unfairly."[14] His comments not only encourage people called to testify before the House Select Committee to remain silent but might also prompt more violence among Trump supporters. It certainly reinforces the open defiance of Trump's leading political advisers, such as Kevin McCarthy, Jim Jordan, and Mark Meadows, in refusing to cooperate with the select committee. John Dean, former Nixon White House counsel, is right in calling Trump's promise of pardons for Capitol rioters "the stuff of dictators," while stressing that "failure to confront a tyrant only encourages bad behavior."[15]

Trump loyalists who have claimed the Capitol thugs were "political prisoners" got a boost from the Republican National Committee in 2022. The RNC gave new meaning to moral depravity when it censured Representatives Liz Cheney (R-WY) and Adam Kinzinger (R-IL) for rebuking Trump's lawless behavior. Moreover, it "declared that the Jan. 6 attack on the U.S. Capitol, unleashed by then President Donald Trump, was merely a situation in which 'ordinary citizens engaged in legitimate political discourse'."[16] The discourse being referred to included threats to hang Mike Pence, calls to shoot Nancy Pelosi, and acts of mob violence resulting in over 140 injured Capitol police officers and five dead—four of whom were Trump supporters. Most regrettably, Brian D. Sicknick, a Capitol police officer, was killed. One officer lost the tip of a finger, and others suffered concussions as a result of having their heads smashed in with baseball bats and flag poles.[17] There was nothing "legitimate" or innocent about the discourse at work in producing these assaults. Once again, violence in the United States went into overdrive.

The use and threat of violence and its enactment have become an entrenched constant among many Republican Party politicians and their followers. How else to explain the defense by most Republicans of the Capitol insurrection as "a patriotic attempt to protect the nation against its enemies."[18] The normalization of violence by the mainstream Republican Party is fully visible in the silence of its members in light of Trump's comment "suggesting that members of Hilary Clinton's 2016 campaign had spied on him and that 'in a stronger period of time in our country, this crime would have been punishable by death.'"[19] This threat was echoed on Fox & Friends by Representative Jim Jordan (R-OH), who "agreed with Trump ... and implied the punishment for such alleged espionage should be death."[20]

Such comments suggest not only that the Republican Party is normalizing violence, but that such violence is a central element of an ascending fascist politics that the Party now embraces without apology. Increasingly, such threats are being put into policy. How can reason and justice prevail in a society when Republican Governor DeSantis in Florida provides macho-infused vigilantes in the aftermath of the Kyle Rittenhouse acquittal a legal pass to shoot, if not kill, peaceful protesters?[21] How else to clarify the rise of deadly misogynist violence, operating under the discourse of surveillance and vigilantism, that has moved from Texas to the law of the land, subjecting women to an incriminating reality that dictates that they are second-class citizens who can no longer have control over their reproductive rights.[22] Violence now offers a lurid fascination and source of emotional satisfaction for the populist voices of extremism that make up a sizable number of the modern Republican Party, revealing the moral abyss inhabited by many of them.

How does one account for the images of guns being celebrated on social media by crazed Republicans, as if the spectacle of violence does not present a danger to a larger public? In one telling instance, US congressman Thomas Massie of Kentucky "posted a Christmas picture of himself and what appears to be his family, smiling and posing with an assortment of guns, just days after four teenagers were killed in a shooting at a high school in Michigan." Accompanying the image was the tweet, "Merry Christmas! ps. Santa, please bring ammo."[23] The image is more than insensitive; it endorses a hyped-up version of gun culture while maximizing the pleasure potentially produced by an obsession with guns and the threat of violence (after all, it was intended as a virtual Christmas card). What Republican Massie mimics in his Christmas family photo is an echo of the cruelty and pornographic fascination and celebration of the spectacle of violence central to fascist politics. This fusing of pleasure, moral irresponsibility, and cruelty legitimatizes the horror of violent acts, including threats of violence as a political weapon to be used against opponents and critics. The image is symptomatic of a moral and political depravity that defines the modern Republican Party and its obsession with violence, fear, and death.

It is no longer an exaggeration to state that violence defines the very essence of politics and increasingly has become a routine element of everyday life. School shootings have become an everyday occurrence, further accelerated by Republican legislators who argue that anyone should be able to buy as many guns as they want, regardless of the danger gun violence poses to the public. As blood flows in the corridors of malls, schools, synagogues, and houses of worship, right-wing Republicans talk more openly in violent terms, threatening their opponents with the use of force and mobilizing their followers with a call for armed confrontation.

Unsurprisingly, one revealing and increasingly symptomatic incident occurred in October 2021 at a conservative rally in Western Idaho. A young man stepped up to a microphone and asked, "When do we get to use the guns" to start killing Democrats; the audience applauded. He then asked, "How many elections are they going to steal before we kill these people?" Lisa Lerer and Astead Herndon reported that "the local state representative, a Republican, later called it a 'fair' question."[24] The racist spirit of the Ku Klux Klan and a politics of racial cleansing have merged with the unchecked greed and systemic violence of a Second Gilded Age to create a rebranded fascist politics that has become normalized in the current counter-revolutionary era.

Former President Trump has brought a wrecking ball to democracy. His embrace of lawlessness provides a cover for injecting violence into politics. In the spirit of this climate of lawlessness, Trump called on his followers at the Texas rally to protest in the streets if he gets indicted, a statement that offered more than a patina of menace. He also stated that then-Vice President Pence was wrong to accept the rightful electors, publicly admitting that he was an active participant in trying to overturn the election. Will Bunch, writing in *The Philadelphia Inquirer,* stated that Trump's speech was "one of the most incendiary and most dangerous speeches in America's 246-year history."[25] He adds another twist to Trump's promise to pardon people who stormed the Capitol in his name and is worth quoting at length:

> It included an appeal for all-out mayhem in the streets to thwart the U.S. justice system and prevent Trump from going to jail, as the vise tightens from overlapping criminal probes in multiple jurisdictions. And it also featured a stunning campaign promise— that Trump would look to abuse the power of the presidency to pardon those involved in the Jan. 6 insurrection ... while Biden is seeking to restore democratic norms, a shadow ex-president— unpunished so far for his role in an attempted coup on Jan. 6— is rebuilding a cult-like movement in the heartland of America, with all the personal grievance and appeals to Brownshirts-style violence that marked the lowest moments of the 20th century. On the 89th anniversary of the date (Jan. 30, 1933) that Adolf Hitler—rehabilitated after his attempted coup—assumed power in Germany, are we repeating the past's mistakes of complacency and underestimation?[26]

Trump's speech does more than offer pardons to January 6 insurrectionists; it also sets the stage for multiple insurrections and deepens a reactionary counter-revolutionary movement, given his call for mob action in those cities where charges may be lodged against him for various illegal actions. Well aware that he might be indicted for multiple crimes, Trump replayed his January 6 speech to the audience in Texas by "Calling for the biggest protests we have ever had" in Atlanta, Washington, and New York City. He further whipped up his base by claiming, "These prosecutors are vicious, horrible people. They're racists and they're very sick—they're mentally sick. They're going after me without any protection of my rights from the Supreme Court or most other courts. In reality, they're not after me, they're after you."[27] It is important to note that these incendiary comments included his use of the term "racist prosecutors." A term aimed at three of the key Black prosecutors investigating Trump and served without shame as a dog whistle and ominous appeal to white supremacists. Bunch writes:

> [i]t's both alarming and yet utterly predictable that Trump would toss the gasoline of racial allegations onto his flaming pile of grievances, knowing how that will play with the Confederate

flag aficionados within the ex-president's cult. In tying skin color into his call for mobs in Atlanta or New York, Trump is seeking to start a race war—no different, really, from Dylann Roof. Roof used a .45-caliber Glock handgun, while Trump uses a podium and the services of fawning right-wing cable TV networks. Sadly, the latter method could prove more effective.[28]

What ties all of these incidents of violence together—whether it be an attack on dissent, women's abortion rights, voting rights, and social justice—is the power and influence of the growing repressive educational forces that serve to depoliticize people and normalize a culture of violence. It is worth repeating that the forces of authoritarianism are deepened and extended throughout American society through an image-based culture of manufactured ignorance and an overcharged cult of lies produced in right-wing cultural apparatuses, toxic social media spheres, and in widely televised attacks on public and higher education. The latter constitute a new public sphere of enormous pedagogical influence that is overlooked among theorists commenting critically on the decline of democracy in the United States and the rise of fascist politics.

Consider the response of the mass media and the Republican Party to the endless occurrence of mass shootings in the United States. The general response is to focus momentarily on the violence largely through personal accounts of grief, buttressed by the call to pray for the victims. Only to be ignored within a week or two following the horrific acts of violence. Within a short time, more mass shootings occur only to be followed by the same personalized and depoliticized commentaries. For example, once the cameras left the scenes of mass shootings in Buffalo, New York, Uvalde, Texas, and Highland Park, Chicago, there were few attempt to address how such violence has become a systemic element of gangster capitalism and its gun culture, how politicians are complicit with the conditions that produce such violence, and how greed and profit are valued more than human life, contributing to rise of the United States as an armed and violent society. Commenting on the aftermath of the shooting at Tops Supermarket in Buffalo, New York, India Walton, a nurse and progressive activist, rightly notes that the media controls the narrative following mass shootings and that once the news cameras leave, the conditions that caused the violence are both overlooked and normalized.[29] As such, violence is reduced to a spectacle, and there is little interest in addressing the underlying forces at work in the United States producing the plague of mass and everyday violence. In this instance, politics under fascism becomes theater. The consequences are deadly, literally and symbolically.

As I have stressed repeatedly in this book, at the heart of this emerging rehabilitated fascism is a politics aggressively at work in the struggle over consciousness, identity, subjectivity, values, and agency. Matters of agency are particularly important because they highlight the ideological forces and material conditions that either enable or limit the ability of individuals within specific economic, political, and social contexts to learn how to use knowledge, values, and power to shape the conditions that define their everyday lives. Agency when depoliticized reduces politics to the realm of subjectivity. As Paul Street observes, "Public knowledge is a matter of life and death," particularly when it is conditioned to offer little resistance to "the political hurricane of white nationalist authoritarianism—fascism, American-style—[that] is bearing down on the United States today."[30] Unfortunately, the current political commentary gives far too little attention to the subjective and cultural conditions that have ushered in modernized forms of fascism in the United States.

CHAPTER NINE

Weaponizing Culture

Sycophantic right-wing cable networks have repeatedly endorsed, if not celebrated, Trump's criminogenic behavior, made visible in his public calls to obstruct justice, his unapologetic misuse of the constitutional power of a presidential pardon for his political allies, and his incendiary racist remarks. America is at war with itself, signaling not just the collapse of both conscience and civil order but also the toxic emergence of a racialized neoliberal culture that is disseminated through popular culture and right-wing cultural apparatuses with the speed of an uncontrolled wildfire. Right-wing media has become an enforcer of the Party line and a powerful disseminator of what Ralph Nader aptly calls micro-repressions, broadcasting daily "zillions of ugly, vicious, and anonymous rants over the internet enabled by the profiteering social media corporations like Facebook."[1] The right-wing media has, with few exceptions, created a safe space for the "big lie" racism, conspiracy theories, and "a hideous ecstasy of fear, and vindictiveness."[2] It is no exaggeration to argue that the right-wing propaganda machine is an "infernal machine of political and human destruction."[3] Jonathan Crary is right in arguing that the internet and the numerous digital landscapes it has spawned under gangster capitalism have become toxic and imposes damaging consequences. He writes:

> The digital tools and services used by people everywhere are subordinated to the power of transnational corporations, intelligence agencies, criminal cartels, and a sociopathic billionaire elite. For the majority of the earth's population on

whom it has been imposed, the internet complex is the implacable engine of addiction. Loneliness, false hopes, cruelty, psychosis, indebtedness, squandered life, the corrosion of memory, and social disintegration. All of its touted benefits are rendered irrelevant or secondary by its injurious and sociocidal impacts.[4]

In the current historical moment, right-wing social media and the internet have become turbo-charged vehicles of hate and censorship controlled largely by anti-democratic forces and a financial elite. As Thomas Klikauer and Meg Young point out, between 2019 and mid-2021, there was a "highly disturbing upsurge in internet-based hate speeches."[5] During that period, there was "a new post about race or hate speech every 1.7 seconds in the US and UK."[6] Klikauer and Young focus on a report covering this time period in *Ditch the Label*. The report pointed to a 28 percent increase in racist and ethnic hate speech, while anti-Asian hate speech increased by an unprecedented 1,662 percent. Furthermore, homophobic hate speech constituted about 85 percent of online conversations. The fusillade of hate speech increased dramatically with the rise of a number of anti-racist movements after the killing of George Floyd. Klikauer and Young rightly note that language is not innocent, and hate speech has had a dangerous impact on society, leading to "real attacks."[7] As they rightly assert, "In short, the path from online violence to 'real world' violence is often rather short."[8]

Censorship now operates across a range of sites including schools, libraries, and screen culture. In addition, Republican legislators have passed laws in a number of states that criminalize various forms of protests. It is against this widespread assault on freedom of speech that the new McCarthyism embraced by the social media has to be understood and engaged. As Chris Hedges and others have noted, censorship against left critics has increasingly become the preferred weapon of the giants of social media such as Twitter, Google, YouTube, and Facebook.

One egregious example took place when YouTube eliminated without prior notice six years of Chris Hedges' popular and critical show, Contact. This was a show that "gave a voice to writers and dissidents, including Noam Chomsky and Cornel West, as well as activists from Extinction Rebellion, Black Lives Matter, third parties and the prison abolitionist movement."[9] In this new form of digital McCarthyism, dominant social media platforms either ban oppositional critics along with critical media outlets, or their traffic is severely limited. Hedges elaborates on the effects of one instance of censorship with much wider implications regarding the banning of critical platforms. He writes:

> Sites that once attracted tens or hundreds of thousands of followers suddenly saw their numbers nosedive. Google's "Project Owl," designed to eradicate "fake news," employed "algorithmic updates to surface more authoritative content" and downgrade "offensive" material. Traffic fell for sites such as Alternet by 63%, Democracy Now by 36%, Common Dreams by 37%, Truthout by 25%, The Intercept by 19% and Counterpunch by 21%. The World Socialist Web site saw its traffic fall by two-thirds. Julian Assange and WikiLeaks were all but erased. Mother Jones editors in 2019 wrote that they suffered a sharp decline in its Facebook audience, which translated to an estimated loss of $600,000 over 18 months.[10]

Hedges' critique of the new digital platforms is important, particularly in how it makes critical ideas and certain authors disappear, but it needs to go further. What also must be analyzed is how a new techno rationality in these media platforms produces new forms of propaganda, legitimates the notion of digital superiority, and intensifies class inequities. Building on the work of Theodor Adorno and Herbert Marcuse, David Berry argues that digital media has produced more powerful forms of instrumental rationality, which reorient thinking itself for the worse, make difficult thoughts disappear, and neutralize opposition by privatizing it.[11] Digital rationality also introduces and legitimates positivist notions of calculation, empiricism, and efficiency as progressive cultural forms that attempt to change daily life and behavior patterns through a reorienting of reason in the name of digital superiority.

Violence finds new pathways in a cultural war machine that has refashioned the link among power, everyday life, and the new communication technologies. Under such conditions, political agency is no longer shaped through traditional public spheres wedded to democratic values. New political and pedagogical formations rooted in savage market principles, a war culture, widespread militarization, a regressive individualism, rigid hedonism, and white supremacy now define the values, identities, social relations, and modes of community consistent with a fascist politics. Under this powerful web of disimagination machines, agency is not simply being refigured, it is being denied its fullest moral and political capacities. Not only are freedom of the press and speech under assault, but democracy and all the institutions that support it are being threatened.

In addition to the current assaults on the freedom of speech, it is crucial to recognize that the political currency of racism is also being accelerated by right-wing media apparatuses in conjunction with the ongoing effort to eliminate the thinking subject and the capacity of people to separate truth from falsehoods. The counter-revolutions emerging in "slow-motion" in America are primarily race wars that reinvigorate class wars, wars against women's reproductive rights, and the war waged against the poor, young people, and immigrants. Again, Goldberg is right in stating that "race-making shapes all the diving modes of civil warring constituting modern politics today. Race-making helps to both to shape and to sharpen them."[12] Not surprisingly, while the Republican Party embraces white supremacy and the struggle for mastery as central to its politics, it works hard to erase the history that informs this racialized state of war. Historical amnesia lays the groundwork for "infrastructures of systemic violence."[13] At work here are the workings of what Michel Foucault once called the "suicidal state," whose purpose is to falsify history in order to sabotage democracy and retool the machineries of the fascist state. It does so by creating a spectral solidarity with the politically corrupt and ethically dead, who resuscitate the ghost of "an absolutely racist State, an absolutely murderous State, and an absolutely suicidal State."[14]

The symbolic realm is increasingly defined by discourses that trade in poisonous beliefs, truth-denying notions of persuasion, historical erasure, and a politics of exclusion. This war-like ocular politics is rooted in a formative culture consumed by violence, narrow-mindedness, and hate.[15] The plague of historical amnesia with its whitewashing of history and its denial of systemic racism symbolizes not only a dread of history but also the right to question it, draw from its resources, hold it accountable, and dream about the possibility for social change by drawing on the repressed lessons of history.

As Hannah Arendt has observed, throughout history totalitarian rulers have attempted to rewrite history in order "to adapt the past to the 'political line' of the present moment, or to eliminate data that did not fit their ideology."[16] The right-wing attack forbidding educators to talk about racial inequities works to erase structural racism and normalize systemic racism. It also suggests how dangerous historical consciousness has become to Trump and his followers, given its possibility to make the real history of America visible. Kimberlé Crenshaw is right in stating that "Not talking about [racial disparities] is simply a way of just naturalizing them, normalizing them, and allowing these patterns to continue over and over again."[17] Moreover, this whitewashing of the curriculum makes visible "the power that education about racism can have on fixing systems of oppression."[18]

The control of images and speech is not limited to right-wing media since such control is also shared by a corporate-owned, mainstream media that trades in propaganda, and echoes many of the characteristics cited by Hannah Arendt in her famous essay "Lying in Politics," written after the Pentagon Papers appeared in 1971.[19] This is particularly true of her claim that facts had become meaningless when assembled in narratives that disregard evidence, the truth, and slide into what she calls an "Alice-in-Wonderland atmosphere." Arendt's claim that America's penchant for lying as a political tool created a kind of collective psychosis in which the "distinction between truth and falsehood, between fact and fantasy ... disappears" is no less true today than when it was written.[20]

In its updated form, lying in politics is driven by an image-making culture, what Arendt termed an "imaginary enterprise," in which the power of manufactured ignorance and the deliberate lie are more powerful than ever, especially given the rise of digital culture and the social media.[21] This merging of power, culture, technology, and everyday life make it easier for falsehoods to prevail and standards disappear. Lying is no longer limited to the realm of public relations, it is now at the center of an image-based politics. Under such circumstances, the culture of lying has become spectacularized, transforming the public sphere into an oversized theater. What Daniel Boorstin once called the "thicket of unreality" in *The Image: or, What Happened to the American Dream* has become in the post-Trump era an organized principle of manufactured ignorance and criminality.

The culture of historical amnesia and immediacy is greatly amplified by a range of cultural apparatuses that have been constructed out of the merging of power and new teaching machines such as Google, Twitter, Facebook, Instagram, and other platforms. As I mention throughout this book, these platforms have become powerful weapons not only for censoring critical ideas but also for spreading lies and misinformation. Culture war politics and the apparatuses that produce its messages are more powerful today than ever before. Dominant practices of representation move easily through the corporate-controlled right-wing electronic media on a variety of sites, working to influence particular forms of reception and secure particular identities and desires. They have become the new cultural pathways for waging a counter-revolution and turning politics into a battleground for launching multiple acts of aggression while furthering a cultural politics that takes on the spirit of a civil war.

As noted in Chapter 8, civil war has taken on the logic of a war culture that defines a politics driven by oppressive forms of popular culture, political education, and exaggerated fears. Civil war defined in purely militaristic terms too often ignores the cultural apparatuses, educational forces, and propagandistic tools used to normalize state-sanctioned violence, permanent war, the weaponization of ignorance, and the pedagogical practices used to create the agents in support of bringing democracy to the point of no return. Trump's January 30 speech at a rally in Texas does more than suggest that the Republican Party is waging a "slow-motion" insurrection; it mimics a politics that fascists from Hitler to Pinochet used in preparing the conditions for violent counter-revolutions. As Steven Monacelli observed in *Rolling Stone*, what took place in Texas is a revival of fascist politics that "demonstrates the sort of far-right politics that is coalescing here: paranoid, obsessed with or tolerant of bigoted conspiracy theories, eager to appeal to violence, and convinced they're fighting against a secret Marxist plot. If this sounds familiar, it's because similar politics emerged during the Weimar period in Germany, were honed by the Nazis, and later trafficked into mainstream politics via the John Birch Society."[22]

This is no exaggeration. In fact, what is astounding about this civil war climate is that threats of violence are being made openly in front of large audiences, on powerful media platforms, and in local shopping areas. For instance, Newt Gingrich, a major adviser to the Congressional Republicans, threatened jail time for committee members investigating the January 6 assault.[23] It should also be noted that ranking right-wing Congressional members unapologetically trade in violent rhetoric. In what seems unthinkable in the United States, neo-Nazis openly demonstrated in Orlando, Florida. Standing near a shopping mall, they were videotaped with swastika flags, chanting "White Power" and "Heil Hitler," "yelling obscene antisemitic insults at people driving by, and mockingly urging them to call police."[24] They also assaulted a driver who left his car to confront them. In the current polarizing environment, this is not altogether surprising.

What is startling is that neo-Nazis and other extremist groups feel empowered to no longer hide in the shadows but brazenly display their racism and hatred openly in public, with little fear of retribution. Unsurprisingly, Republican Florida Gov. Ron DeSantis failed to respond quickly enough to the event, and when he did, he used the occasion to claim that Democrats were using the event as a political issue to smear him. The editorial board of the *Miami Herald* suggested that DeSantis' refusal to immediately condemn the Nazi demonstrators served to give them cover. The governor's press secretary appeared to prove the point when she responded to the event, suggesting the group may not have even been Nazis. Her remarks were widely condemned. This is more than a display of ethical irresponsibility in full bloom; it is symptomatic of how far right-wing extremism now occupies the centers of political power, while they are willing to display their fascist politics as a badge of honor.

CHAPTER TEN

Gangster Capitalism and the Politics of Ethicide

Barbara F. Walter, the author of *How Civil Wars Start*, states that "Most people don't realize they are on the path to civil war until the violence is a feature of everyday life."[1] Implied in her insightful comment is that long before violence becomes normalized in society, politics descends into ethicide—a collective disavowal of social responsibility and the removal of political, discursive, and economic actions from any sense of the social costs involved. Ethicide is at the heart of the Republican Party's embrace of a counter-revolution, whose purpose is the destruction of any vestige of democracy and the institutions that support it. Central to the politics of ethicide is a removal of ethical boundaries, resulting in what Joshua Sperling defines as "The blunting of the senses; the hollowing out of language; the erasure of connection with the past, the dead ... possibly, too, the erasure even of certain emotions, whether pity, compassion, consoling, mourning, or hoping."[2]

The coupling of racial hatred and a politics of exclusion with the espousal of political violence is the sharpest expression of America's turn toward a modernized form of authoritarianism and a counter-revolutionary politics increasingly defined as an expression of civil war. As Theodor Adorno has suggested in his analysis of right-wing extremism, what is at work in this GOP view of counter-revolution is a fascist politics that "feeds off apocalyptic fantasies" not unlike those that could be "found among the Nazi leadership."[3] White vigilantism is no longer on the fringes of American society.

America's Nazi problem is rooted in a lengthy past of fascist ideologies and the racist actions of a slave state, the racist violence espoused by the Ku Klux Klan, and a historical era that constitutes what Alberto Toscano calls "the long shadow of racial fascism."[4] Fascist politics is no longer in the shadows in spite of the Republican's attempt to erase its historical and racial dynamics in the United States. As Noam Chomsky has observed, the United States is not experiencing a drift toward a newly revised form of fascism, "it is underway right now."[5] In fact, as the historian Sarah Churchwell observes, many of fascism's most conspicuous elements are on display in the United States and unapologetically embraced in the era of Trumpism. She states:

> conspicuous features [of fascism] are recognizably shared, including: nostalgia for a purer, mythic, often rural past; cults of tradition and cultural regeneration; paramilitary groups; the delegitimizing of political opponents and demonization of critics; the universalizing of some groups as authentically national, while dehumanizing all other groups; hostility to intellectualism and attacks on a free press; anti-modernism; fetishized patriarchal masculinity; and a distressed sense of victimhood and collective grievance. Fascist mythologies often incorporate a notion of cleansing, an exclusionary defense against racial or cultural contamination, and related eugenicist preferences for certain "bloodlines" over others. Fascism weaponizes identity, validating the Herrenvolk and invalidating all the other folk.[6]

None of this appears out of the ordinary in the current historical moment, suggesting, as Coco Das points out, that America has a Nazi problem.[7] At the same time, it is essential to stress that I am not suggesting that the former Trump administration was a precise replica of Hitler's Nazi Germany. Yet, as Churchwell and a number of historians, writers, and critics have argued, there are important parallels that cannot be ignored.[8] Fascism has deep roots in American history, and its basic elements can crystalize in different forms under unique historical circumstances. Rather than being a replica of the past, fascism should be viewed as a series of patterns that emerge out of different conditions that produce what Hannah Arendt called totalitarian forms. These patterns are especially obvious as the modern Republican Party's attempts to engage in forms of historical erasure and racial cleansing, coupled with its insidious efforts to define calls for racial justice as forms of racial hatred. It is precisely this twisted logic that is used to cast white men as victims of reverse racism.[9]

As the late Daniel Guerin, one of the more authoritative experts on fascism, made clear there is no single version of fascism, "there are many fascisms."[10] Fascism is not interred strictly in a specific history, and its different histories are critical to understand because it mutates, evolves, and often lies dormant, but it never goes away. The potential for fascism exists in every society, and its histor(ies) teach us that there is much to lose if we fail to learn its lessons.[11] There is no perfect fit between 1930s Germany and Trump and his followers in the current era, but there are alarming echoes of Nazism's sordid history.

As I have argued in Chapter 5, the threat of fascism is especially acute under neoliberalism, which exacerbates the worst elements of gangster capitalism. This includes most emphatically the widening of the scourge of inequality, a looming economic crisis, a contempt for social responsibility, the promotion of racial hatred, a growing ecological catastrophe, the acceleration of a politics of disposability, a corrupt alignment with big business, the destruction of labor unions, and a belief in the necessity of a heroic leader.[12] Peter Dolack is right in arguing that while "militarism, extreme nationalism, the creation of enemies and scapegoats" are basic elements of a fascist politics, "the most critical component is a rabid propaganda that intentionally raises panic and hate while disguising its true nature and intentions under the cover of a phony populism." He concludes by stating that "As long as capitalism exists, the threat of fascism exists."[13] This may be an understatement. If anything, the United States may be well beyond the threat.[14]

The American model of fascism is rooted in an unapologetic acceptance of exceptionalism and a robust militarism, on the one hand, and a marriage of white supremacy and predatory neoliberal capitalism on the other.[15] The charter elements of this racial exceptionalism and call for national renewal were evident in Trump's speech at his Save America rally just before the Capitol was attacked. In his remarks, he argued that America's way of life was up for grabs, it is in a state of decline, and the time had come to save it at any cost, and only American patriots "can take back our country."[16] Today, economic exceptionalism and racial terrorism are connected and drive a Republican Party that is relentless in its destruction of the rights of Black people and its willingness to hollow out democratic institutions.

While references to fascism gained more visibility among liberals and some conservatives in the aftermath of the failed Capitol coup, they largely characterized Trump and his policies rather than the fascist history that informed them.[17] In other instances, a number of liberal historians and academics went out of their way to disassociate either Trump or his regime from the mobilizing passions of a fascist politics.[18] Moreover, while a range of legal experts such as Lawrence H. Tribe and political scientists such as Professor Robert Pape believe that democracy is in danger, they refuse to accept that the United States is on the brink of fascism understood within the context of a savage expansion of neoliberal capitalism.[19] Increasingly, as the threat of fascism becomes more dangerous, liberals such as *New York Times* columnist Paul Krugman and noted writers such as Francine Prose believe that comparing the current state of American politics with the rise of fascism is not acceptable. What they do acknowledge is euphemistically labeled as rule by minority government and the seeds of autocracy. In the end, this type of refusal to name the fascist threat borders on being complicit with the rebranded forms of fascism they refuse to acknowledge.[20] What is missed in these arguments is how the legacies of fascism emerge in diverse forms in different societies and the potential stranglehold this rebranded form of American fascism has on the future. What we are witnessing in the United States is not merely a threat to democracy but a modernized and dangerous expression of right-wing extremism that amounts to a full-blown version of fascist politics.

PART THREE

The Public Imagination under Siege

CHAPTER ELEVEN

Cultural Apparatuses and the Politics of Commonsense

In this chapter, I analyze the pedagogical politics at work in those corporate-controlled cultural apparatuses that have become tools of intellectual domination under neoliberal capitalism. I argue that central to such a task is an understanding and further theorizing of the role that commonsense has come to play as a legitimating pedagogical tool that now circulates through various cultural pathways, including schools.

Transnational corporations have developed what Crary calls an internet complex of "intelligence agencies" and disimagination machines that qualify as: "engines of addiction, loneliness, false hopes cruelty, psychosis, indebtedness ... and social disintegration."[1] Toni Morrison provides an example of the link between fascism and such disimagination machines in an article she wrote in *The Journal of Negro Education* in 1995. At that time, Morrison noted that "Fascism can only be supported by an environment that supports its growth."[2] She further states that fascism gains its power through the creation of a formative culture, whose purpose is to market identities, subjectivities, and values, producing "the perfect capitalist."[3] She concludes by observing that fascism colonizes the mind, spirit, and courage:

> When our fears have all been serialized, our creativity censored, our ideas "marketplaced," or rights sold, our intelligence

sloganized, our strength downsized, our privacy auctioned; when the theatricality, the entertainment value, the marketing of life is complete, we will find ourselves living not in a nation but in a consortium of industries, and wholly unintelligible to ourselves except for what we see as through a screen darkly.[4]

Central to Morrison's argument is that fascism thrives on the breakdown of shared values and becomes normalized by creating a cultural politics and modes of commonsense that subvert language, agency, truth, and democracy. In this sense, fascism is not only a consequence of the breakdown of democracy and a failed neoliberal capitalist economy but also of the failure of language, shared beliefs, rationality, and the power of truth. In addition, there is the destruction and collapse of civic culture and cultural politics that creates the ideological and institutional conditions necessary for producing critically engaged citizens. This is especially alarming since there is no democracy without an informed public and no justice without a discourse of injustice.

C. Wright Mills has argued that since everyone is dependent on meaning, education has become central to politics, especially in an age in which the blending of power, culture, and everyday life has amounted to a revolution in the mass production of knowledge, information, and entertainment. Mills points to the pedagogical power in society of what he called cultural apparatuses.[5] Mills' work on the centrality of culture and the cultural apparatuses that support it follows the work of cultural theorists such as Antonio Gramsci and Raymond Williams, and Cornelius Castoriadis. It also builds on Raymond Williams' concept of "permanent education," which stresses "the educational force of our whole social and cultural experience" as a teaching machine.[6] For Mills, the complex of cultural apparatuses in society amounted to a form of public pedagogy, or what we might call vast machineries of persuasion. Defining the emerging cultural apparatuses, he writes:

This apparatus is composed of all the organizations and milieux in which artistic, intellectual, and scientific work goes on, and by which entertainment and information are produced and distributed. It contains an elaborate set of institutions: of schools and theaters, newspapers and census bureau, studios, laboratories, museums, little magazines, radio networks. It contains truly fabulous agencies of exact information and of trivial distraction, exciting objects, lazy escape, and strident advice. Inside this apparatus, standing between men and events, the images, meanings, slogans that define the world in which men live are organized and compared, maintained, and revised, lost and cherished, hidden, debunked, celebrated. It is the source of the Human Variety—of styles of living and of ways to die.[7]

According to Mills, these new corporate-controlled machineries of persuasion—extending from print and audio to visual apparatuses—have been increasingly appropriated by dominant institutional orders, becoming "a close adjunct of national authority and a leading agency of nationalist propaganda."[8] In this case, the merging of state power and right-wing cultural apparatuses created the conditions for controlling the narrative around a range of political and social issues. Of course, there is more at issue here than the mass production of propaganda and misinformation; there is also what Mills calls the expropriation of experience and the horizons of political agency. As Mills writes:

The cultural apparatus not only guides experience; often as well it expropriates the very chance to have experience that can rightly be called "our own." For our standards of credibility, our definitions of reality, our modes of sensibility—as well as our immediate opinions and images—are determined much less by any pristine experience than by our exposure to the output of the cultural apparatus. This apparatus is the seat of civilization, which, in Matthew Arnold's phrase, is "the humanization of man in society." It is in terms of some such conception as this apparatus that the politics of culture may be understood.[9]

Fundamental to Mills' analysis is the idea, stated as well by Vaclav Havel, that politics follows culture and that matters of agency, consciousness, identity, and thinking are the foundation for entering into the world of meaning and politics while providing the conditions for establishing an educated democracy. For Mills, culture was a valuable resource for people to develop a critical awareness of themselves and their relationship to the larger world; it was a central site where critical literacy and the civic imagination could be developed as part of the pedagogical practice of freedom.[10] According to Mills, the practice of freedom signaled the need for self-reflection, bridging the gap between theory and everyday life, and connecting learning to matters of power and difficult knowledge. In fact, he believed that the realms of culture, education, and consciousness might be the most important domains where political struggles are lost and won.

What we have learned from Mills is not only that soft wars are now won through the apparatuses of persuasion, commonsense, and propaganda, but that state power has the upper hand, especially in the United States, in deploying culture as a form of power. What was not evident in Mills' lifetime was the rise of what Crary calls 24/7 capitalism, with its emphasis on speed, frenzy, immediacy, accumulation, extraction, and the collapse of what I call public time—time that makes room for contemplation, dialogue, thoughtfulness, and informed judgment, all the habits crucial for democratic citizenship.[11] As Crary observes, culture is now shaped by the global power of the "internet-complex" with its "numbing online routines" and its undoing of the concrete bonds of solidarity and embodied communities. Agency is no longer simply shaped by this new form of ocular politics personified by the digital media; it is absorbed and integrated into it. Everything, including reality itself, is shaped by what one experiences via screen culture. Framing mechanisms function as powerful pedagogical tools that shape the questions asked, the behavior we enable, and the identities we inhabit. Under such circumstances, conformity, social atomization, the disabling of historical memory, and the commodification of thought itself prefigure both a crisis of agency and the death of democracy as both a promise and ideal.

The Depoliticizing Politics of Commonsense

The struggle over consciousness cannot be separated from the ways in which commonsense operates as a fundamental pedagogical force in removing ideas, values, and social relations from critical analysis. As Antonio Gramsci, Stuart Hall, and Noam Chomsky, among others, have rightly argued, commonsense is the accumulation of learned behavior, especially as it functions through a variety of sources, extending from family, friends, the educational system, and social media, to shape ideas, identities, beliefs, and values.[12] It can contain dominant as well as critical elements—bad sense and good sense—though what both share is an unreflective sense. As Stuart Hall and Alan O' Shea observe,

> Commonsense can be understood as a kind of 'everyday thinking' that offers us frameworks of meaning with which to make sense of the world. It is a form of popular, easily available knowledge that contains no complicated ideas, requires no sophisticated argument, and does not depend on deep thought or wide reading. It works intuitively, without forethought or reflection. It is pragmatic and empirical, giving the illusion of arising directly from experience, reflecting solely the realities of daily life, and answering the needs of 'the common people' for practical guidance and advice.[13]

A primary depoliticizing tenet of the neoliberal project is its attempt to produce language masquerading as commonsense. The most obvious assumption being that society can only be understood as a market, coupled with the fatalistic claim that neoliberal capitalism is beyond any possible modification or intervention. Mark Fischer was right when he wrote in *Capitalist Realism* that capitalism presents itself as the only viable political and economic system, echoing the popular saying that "It is easier to imagine the end of the world than to imagine the end of capitalism." The latter functions not only as a form of emotional and ideological plague but also creates a moral and intellectual void easily filled by hatred for those others who are considered disposable. These assumptions are reinforced given the fact that neoliberal commonsense is reproduced through various disimagination machines that spread a culture of fear, endorse a relentless militarism, naturalize massive inequalities in wealth and power, commercialize everything, and replace the social state with the punishing state.

Commonsense redefines the relationship between power, culture, and pedagogical modes of governance. It makes clear that culture deploys power and, in its most repressive forms, is about securing legitimacy. As a legitimating configuration, commonsense always has unruly moments and has to struggle to impose itself as a set of taken-for-granted assumptions. It is always open to being questioned, ruptured, and delegitimated as a pedagogical force. As a site of struggle, it operates on contradictory grounds that can always be called into question and opens the possibility to lay claim to the power of the imagination and the importance of critical reflection in addressing readymade interpretations.

Commonsense makes clear that politics is educative and that matters of political agency are deeply indebted to pedagogical matters of values, beliefs, and identification. At the very least, given the symbolic power of commonsense to normalize particular ideologies, identities, and social relations, it is imperative for educators and other cultural workers to bear some responsibility for challenging commonsense as a form of hegemonic domination—a kind of ideological amnesia. This suggests addressing the educative power of politics and the power of its persuasiveness in a multiplicity of settings within diverse contexts. It also suggests that cultural workers make sure their attempts to shatter the illusions of unanimity of dominant voices reach a variety of public spheres in a language that people can understand. In this instance, as Raymond Williams insightfully observed, politics must also be understood as a form of learning that makes us both subjects and subject to power.[14]

Central to this argument is the recognition that education is fundamentally political both as an emancipatory force and as a tool of repression.[15] As bell hooks has argued, education can nurture individuals to be independent thinkers and enhance "our capacity to be free" or reinforce the habits of conformity, rituals of control, and obedience to oppressive authority.[16] By recognizing education's dialectical character or double bind, the lines of struggle can be clearly drawn for fighting for critical pedagogical models and practices that function as modes of empowerment that connect civic education, civic values, and political agency.

Critical education, as it has emerged in the long tradition of work that extends from John Dewey, W. E. B. DuBois, and Paulo Freire to Ivan Illich, Pierre Bourdieu, Maxine Greene, and bell hooks, recognizes that it is not only the knowledge, values, and social relationships that matter but also the spaces in which pedagogy operates. As Larry Grossberg has argued: It is in "the space between people's everyday lives and the material production and distribution of values and power, in the space where people and groups are articulated, both ideologically and effective to social identities, cultural practices and political projects ... that pedagogy must operate."[17] If progressives are to address the underlying problems of censorship, alienation, rage, loneliness, and anxiety, education must operate as a central discourse of critique and as an emancipatory force for social change.[18]

This is especially true given that some of the most powerful corporate-controlled conservative cultural apparatuses now trafficking between institutions and authority function as powerful pedagogical sites and provide the conditions and formative cultures in which struggles over agency, identity, and consciousness develop. The right-wing media apparatus is a rage machine the purpose of which is to divide, segregate, dehumanize, and exclude. Rather than deal with the problems produced by capitalism, they displace popular anger. As Richard Wolff observes, they do this in order "to redirect people's desire to protest the economic and social decline impinging on them due to [the] decline of capitalism. This is accomplished by loudly and repeatedly blaming certain scapegoats: immigrants, Black and brown people, secularists, women, and liberals."[19] Trump and his reactionary allies are more than willing to address dissatisfaction and mass anxiety with aspects of capitalism that affect their base, but they do so with fake symbolic gestures that breathe new life into the system. And they find powerful support for their faux anger in the high-stake world of persuasion largely monopolized by the cultural apparatuses that thrive on depravity, vulgarity, and spectacle.

It is worth repeating that the rise of right-wing media disimagination machines, especially talk radio and platforms such as Fox News, are replete with hosts such as Dan Bongino, Glenn Beck, and Tucker Carlson, who spew out lies, insults, and conspiracy theories to an audience of millions in what might be called a savage combative manner.[20] Right-wing talk radio, in particular, has and may continue to be a more reliable measure of the breadth of right-wing populism and the political future.[21] As Evan Osnos points out in a *New Yorker* article about Dan Bongino, a popular right-wing commentator, conservative American talk radio "remains a colossus; for every hour that Americans listened to podcasts in 2021, they listened to six and a half hours of AM/FM radio."[22] Equally disturbing is his comment that talk radio throws gasoline on the fires of potential insurrections in the United States. He writes that if one spends "several months immersed in American talk radio

... you'll come away with the sense that the violence of January 6th was not the end of something but the beginning."[23]

Ideology that is unapologetically hate-filled, anti-intellectual, and demeaning now triumphs over truth, ethics, and social responsibility. Right-wing media is engaged in forms of cultural and bare-knuckled combat the endpoint of which is not just to unite Trump followers and divide critics, but to destroy dissent and civic culture, if not democracy itself.[24] This is especially true of Murdoch owned media, which in order to gain maximum shock and emotional impact, has zealously promoted the ideology of white supremacy. The Murdoch empire has become a criminogenic enterprise willfully producing ignorance, lies, and racial hatred.

Throughout this book, I have stressed the power of social media and other cultural apparatuses, because they have a profound role today in shaping agency, national identity, and meaning. Agency has become a site of intense struggle and highlights the power of political education and cultural politics in producing and managing political agency and subjectivity itself. Matters of identity, agency, and identification are political markers that connect ideology to actions, the marriage of ideas to power, and literacy to an act of intervention. Part of the struggle over agency is to provide individuals with the ideas, skills, and capacities to enable them to free themselves from the prison-house of existing mental structures, give them the opportunity to develop a critical consciousness as an essential precondition for taking control of one's own agency, reclaiming one's history, and enacting social change.

Under neoliberalism, identity has been interiorized, removed from a larger calling, and this has set the stage for both the privatizing of politics and any meaningful understanding of solidarity, public goods, and community. Paul Gilroy is right in stating that under neoliberalism, "Identity has been used to promote an inward turn away from the profane chaos of an imperfect world and culminates in a retreat into an anti-social form of self-scrutiny as a substitute for the promise of public political work."[25] In opposition to such a view, Gilroy calls for modes of agency and identity formation that provide the basis for "political action rather than a substitute for it."[26] The theoretical political possibility for doing so is to be found in creating the ideas, social relations, and formative cultures that emerge out of everyday struggles that connect education to the formation of democratic, engaged political agents.

CHAPTER TWELVE

Anti-Capitalist Consciousness and the Crisis of Education

The current struggle against rising authoritarianism will not succeed unless a multigenerational working-class mass movement emerges. This movement must be willing to create the conditions for developing a collective anti-capitalist consciousness as the basis for radical and democratically inspired forms of resistance. David Harvey is right in arguing that the fundamental problems facing the United States "are actually so deep right now that there is no way that we are going to go anywhere without a very strong anti-capitalist movement."[1] The misery, alienation, hardships, asset stripping, and exploitation central to capitalism are beyond reform. Capitalism and democracy are antithetical to each other and necessitate not only a decoupling of one from the other but also the destruction of the entire general order of capitalist rationality, power, and its commanding symbolic and economic institutions.

As Robin D. G. Kelley has argued, "our survival as a species and as a planet depends on the overthrow of capitalism, the redistribution of wealth, and a complete reordering of society based on collective needs."[2] Capitalism's fundamental antagonisms between wealth and poverty, capital and labor, and compassion and greed are often hidden by those who have power, monopolize knowledge, and control the cultural apparatuses that shape consciousness. This is happening at a "historical moment when class antagonisms are as acute as ever."[3] Crucial to challenging the ideological and iniquitous institutions of gangster capitalism is a rethinking of the language of politics, power, agency, and education. As I have noted, this is particularly critical in an age when book burning, censorship, and a full-scale attack on educators and librarians have formed the central political strategy of a Republican Party controlled by authoritarian extremists. The irony here is that right-wing extremists now argue that democracy is obsolete and want to decouple it from capitalism, but not because capitalism is destructive. Rather, they want to eliminate democracy in order for capitalism to evolve into its most unadulterated expression, which is authoritarianism or what they call illiberal democracy.

Language often fails in the midst of a crisis that upends traditional notions of freedom, politics, and democracy. New and unfamiliar cracks appear in public life. The unthinkable appears on the horizon, and the familiar machinery of politics begins to collapse, producing mass anxiety, fear, and a cultural and political landscape that gives rise to the ballast of long-repressed echoes of authoritarianism. Indifferent to the anti-democratic forces that have shaped its history, much of the American public is unprepared to acknowledge that the country has moved from being under the shadow of a legacy of fascism to being caught in its vice. Any attempt at creating such a language and the strategies it will inform will have to address the importance of an emancipatory formative culture in which matters of cultural politics, popular education, subjectivity, and everyday life become central concerns. Under such circumstances, education must define itself through an emancipatory project in which it assumes a major role and responsibility in addressing injustices, human rights, pressing social problems, and the need for fundamental political and economic change.

Put differently, there is a need to produce a civic culture in which critical education becomes an essential element of social and economic justice, wakefulness, dignity, and agency. The importance of how culture functions formatively to produce democratic modes of agency, desires, and identities highlights the increased centrality of education to politics. Additionally, cultural politics is also a crucial part of the need to create a new language for addressing the role of new networks power associated with the digital revolution and the emergence of new and expanding modes of repression.

The pedagogical force of culture makes clear that political forms of education matter and demand a vision and language in which the call for real change resonates with the concrete needs, desires, values, and modes of identification that working-class people of every stripe can understand and relate to critically. The politics of civic culture cannot be removed from the importance of civic education, which should enable students to consider different points of view and be willing to shift their ways of thinking.

Needless to say, both pedagogy and thinking become dangerous to those wedded to dominant forms of cultural politics and repressive notions of civic life. The degradation of civic culture cannot be understood separately from current attacks on the social contract, critical education, the public imagination, the welfare state, and a civic spirit infused with the promise of a strong democracy. Moreover, the emancipatory possibilities of education lie in infusing it with the spirit of critique, struggle, and a vision in which it plays a central political role in the struggle for democratic socialism. The challenge here is to not only remove civic culture from the language and pedagogy of domination but also to infuse it with modes of civic education infused with the ideals, habits, and social relations that embody political and economic rights, justice and security, critique and possibility. This struggle is especially crucial with regards to the current attacks on public education. Authoritarians such as Governors Ron DeSantis, Gregg Abbott, and Glenn Youngkin have a concerted plan to ban almost any form of critical thought from public education. Teachers as well as progressives and the tepid Democratic Party need to organize themselves and develop a plan to defend public education.

Dangerous extremists such as Florida Gov. DeSantis echo views about public schooling that are supported by the likes of David Duke, the former head of the Ku Klux Klan, not to mention most other right-wing groups. Not only are DeSantis's racist attacks evident in his toxic policies banning the teaching of critical race theory in public schools, but he also has stated that his ban has other targets such as transgender youth, critical academics, librarians, and public school teachers. He made this clear in his comment that "there's a lot of other inappropriate content that can be smuggled in by public schools."[4] One does not have to be a rocket scientist to recognize the latter statement as a threat to any form of learning that is critical, socially relevant, or capable of enabling students to learn the skills necessary to be critically engaged citizens. DeSantis is symptomatic of a counter-revolutionary battle being waged by Republican Party extremists against young people, the imagination, democracy, and the future itself. DeSantis' ultimate goal is to destroy not only public education but any institution defined as a public good.

Any resistance movement must acknowledge that the formative cultures necessary to create modes of education, thought, dialogue, critique, and critical agency—the necessary conditions of any aspiring democracy—have been largely destroyed through the pacification of large segments of the public and the elimination of public spheres capable of creating such a culture. This is especially evident given the Republican Party's efforts, along with conservative groups, to ban progressive books about race, gender, and sexuality from libraries and schools. These include books such as George M. Johnson's "All Boys Aren't Blue," Jonathan Evison's "Lawn Boy," Maia Kobabe's "Gender Queer," and Toni Morrison's "The Bluest Eye."[5] Amplified by right-wing social media, ongoing "attempts to ban books in the United States surged in 2021 to the highest level since the American Library Association began tracking book challenges 20 years ago."[6] Along with efforts to racially whitewash school curricula, some states such as New Hampshire are initiating legislation that "would ban the advocacy of any 'doctrine' or 'theory' promoting a 'negative' account of U.S. history, including the notion that the United States was founded on racism."[7] Additionally, the proposed New Hampshire bill "outlaws advocacy for doctrines such as socialism or Marxism."[8]

Virginia Gov. Glenn Youngkin, taking a lesson from the Stasi, former East Germany's feared Ministry for State Security, has gone so far as to call on parents to rat on schools and teachers who teach "divisive" topics such as racism and other critical social issues.[9] Some school systems are going further by threatening to punish teachers who do not conform to the GOP's rules on censorship and restrictions against teaching "prohibited ideas."[10] In Iowa and Florida, Republican lawmakers would require cameras in every classroom. Parents would be able to access the "videos at any time," in order to ensure that alleged controversial issues are not being taught in classrooms.[11] According to Chris Walker, "Recordings would be livestreamed and available for parents or guardians to watch on the internet at any time. School employees who don't comply with the measure would be fined, facing a deduction from their paycheck of up to 5 percent for each week that they don't abide by the rule."[12] Right-wing attempts at censorship, parading under the notion of parental rights, have taken a page out of the dystopian novel *1984*, in which reading certain books is considered a crime. For instance, as reported by Elizabeth A. Harris and Alexandra Alter in the *New York Times*:

> A county prosecutor's office in Wyoming considered criminal charges against library employees for stocking books such as "This Book is Gay" and "Sex Is a Funny Word." A school board member in Flagler County, Fla., filed a complaint with the sheriff's department against a book called "All Boys Aren't Blue."[13]

Such acts of censorship along with its accompanying pedagogy of coercion are about more than a draconian disregard for teacher and student rights. It is important to note that most of the targeted books being censored by right-wingers focus on Black and LGBTQ individuals, underpinning the importance of white supremacist ideology.[14] Such actions are frighteningly similar to the indoctrination efforts that took place in Nazi Germany, practices that embraced an education rooted in racial cleansing and "changed the education system so that resistance to fascist ideas were kept to a minimum."[15] One of the lessons of history that cannot be forgotten is that the indoctrination efforts that took place in Nazi Germany did more than produce a mode of education and language dedicated to burning books that encouraged decadence and moral depravity.[16] It laid the foundation for creating a society of monsters that soon afterward not only burned books but also bodies.

Make no mistake. The current attack on public schools and controversial issues aims at both destroying education as a democratic and critical public sphere and whitewashing history and knowledge in the interests of white supremacist values and ideas. The right-wing attack on education is part of a broader attempt to both privatize it and turn it into "dead zones of the imagination," reduced to anti-public spheres whose aim is to eliminate critical thinking and reasoning, civic literacy, and historical memory.[17] As sites of pedagogical repression, schools are now being conditioned to conform, disavow critical analytical skills, and disavow any respect for democracy, justice, and what it might mean to connect learning to social change. Bell hooks is right in arguing there is nothing less at stake in this attack on critical thinking and public education than the very nature of democratic education itself. She writes:

> the future of democratic education will be determined by the extent to which democratic values can triumph over the spirit of oligarchy that seeks to silence diverse voices, prohibit free speech, and deny citizens access to education ... democracy thrives in an environment where learning is valued, where the ability to think is the mark of responsible citizenship, where free speech and the will to dissent is accepted and encouraged.[18]

There is more at work than a hysterical moral panic over controversial issues being taught in schools. This is a systemic and dangerous attempt by right-wing extremists to use schools to produce an authoritarian culture that stifles creative thinking, problem-solving, informed judgment, and critical learning in classrooms, all in the name of allegedly preventing students from feeling uncomfortable. The call to ensure that students do not feel uncomfortable in the classroom is code for eliminating the tension that comes with refusing to live in a circle of certainty; it is the refusal to enable students to inhabit that space of confrontation between what is and what ought to be—a space that is important to acknowledge when one addresses the need for social change.

Making comfort a foundational element of education is a prescription for a politics of adjustment, conformity, and the refusal to take risks. Being comfortable as a principle of learning is nothing less than a call to deaden the critical faculties and imagination, and accept the world as it is—a lethal refusal to consider other possibilities. The actual purpose of this pedagogy of repression and conformity is to abolish the realm of critical thought, eliminate a culture of critical inquiry, and prevent students from recognizing and resisting anti-democratic forms of power. In this scenario, thinking is recognized as a threat to the status quo, and the institutional and pedagogical conditions that encourage it are viewed with contempt and derision. Cleansing teaching and students of any critical impulses is imperative for a right-wing movement and Republican

Party that trades in manufactured ignorance and mass stupidity as a mode of political control.

What is disturbing about this attack is how liberals utterly misrecognize both the political nature of education and how as a site of struggle it has largely been reduced to nothing more than a corporate and ideological workstation for training a compliant and conformist labor force, not to mention its role as a social sorting machine. Liberals such as George Packer decry politics entering education when, in fact, it is impossible to separate education from matters of power, inequality, racism, neoliberal austerity, the forces of commodification, privatization, and corporate influence—forces that define education as an ongoing site of struggle and politics.[19] He is either indifferent or uninformed about who controls the narratives that shape the curricula and determine which knowledge, values, and classroom social relations are considered most worthwhile. Matters of power and politics disappear in his narrative about education, and as such he has nothing to say about the context in which educators use their authority to shape their students' identities and legitimate certain forms of agency over others. Or how the state and other political interests deskill teachers in order to limit their control over their working conditions. He ignores matters concerning the relationship between knowledge and power, and how education is connected not simply to the acquisition of knowledge but also agency and visions of the future.

Packer and other aligned liberals seem to think that both the left and right have somehow equally politicized the alleged unsullied and innocent space of public education.[20] This false equivalency is telling, because it fails to acknowledge the neoliberal assault by liberals and conservatives that has been going on since the late 1970s. This repressive turn in public and higher education ushered in a period of deadening instrumental rationality, a mania of teaching for the test, an expansion of corporate values, and what Peter Fleming calls an educational system that "tends towards authoritarianism, sometimes overt, often hidden but always experienced as pointlessly excessive by its recipients."[21] If the left calls for schools to function as democratic public spheres infused with the merging of excellence and equity, the right has done just the opposite, turning them into social sorting machines, banning books, and doing everything it can to destroy them as viable public goods. To equate the influence of the left and right on education is more than a misrecognition; it is an egregious act of deception.

Packer along with many of his liberal and conservative allies often defend their respective positions by appealing to balance, objectivity, and other related abstractions, which in reality, as Stanley Fish has argued, is nothing less than an empty politics of avoidance and "is a strategy and as such is always political." He goes further and states:

> In that way no one can accuse you of endorsing or saying or meaning anything. Doing the dance of balance indemnifies you from any criticism, except the criticism that you stand for nothing in particular, which will hardly be received as criticism given that standing for something particular, or being perceived to stand for something particular, is what you are trying to avoid.[22]

Jamelle Bouie provides a different perspective on politics and education and is on target in claiming that the purpose of the "dangerous censoriousness pulsing through American society [is to] suppress debate and stifle discussion in favor of the rote memorization of approved facts."[23] He further argues that

> Free speech, free discourse and free debate are among the great traditions of this country. They are, at this moment, under threat from a well-organized, well-funded movement of right-wing ideologues who have used both the force of the mob and their own institutional power (including that of the state itself) to impose their edicts on [education and] the public at large.[24]

For all the blustering by the right-wing about the need for balance, there is, as the legendary reporter Carl Bernstein points out, the fact that "The Truth is not neutral."[25] But there is more to be concerned about than the right-wing's crude appeals to balance while engaging in naked acts of censorship and promoting a culture of imagination-killing conformity. Such attacks on critical education create a climate of fear and intimidation designed to strike anxiety and silence in teachers in order to control them. Fearing that a student or parent might complain about what is said or taught in class, teachers err on the side of caution or self-censor themselves in order to avoid a public battle or lose their jobs.[26] Amanda Marcotte, reporting on the chilling effects on teachers pushed by the reactionary "Moms for Liberty," puts it well. According to Marcotte:

> To protect their jobs, many teachers may simply skip over lessons on slavery, Jim Crow, or the civil rights movement. That's the clear goal of groups like Moms for Liberty. They want to indoctrinate children with a fake American history that pretends those things never happened. [They want to intimidate] teachers from ever talking about the history of American racism.[27]

Republican politicians in forty-two states have instituted laws governing how race can be restricted and taught.[28] This highly political offensive is aimed at preventing teachers and students from being exposed to what the far-right calls "a liberal agenda," which is a convenient fiction for any issue that deals critically with matters of history, systemic racism, social justice, and sexual orientation. This attack aims to depoliticize and deskill teachers and students by removing matters of politics, power, and equity from the classroom. When critical thought, self-reflection, informed dialogue, and a range of opinions are banned from the classroom, agency is diminished, citizen skills wane, and depoliticization becomes normalized. Richard Corcoran, the former Florida education commissioner, made this reactionary stance clear when he pointed out in a speech, as reported by Laura Meckler and Hannah Natanson, that it was necessary to '"police' teachers to make sure they are not indoctrinating students with a liberal agenda ... I've censored or fired or terminated numerous teachers. There was an entire classroom memorialized to Black Lives Matter and we made sure [the teacher] was terminated."[29]

The right-wing agenda at work in this depoliticizing machinery of censorship was evident following a resolution by the Faculty Council at the University of Texas at Austin rejecting any outside political interference in dictating what could be taught, including matters of race and social justice. In a tweet, Texas Lt. Gov. Dan Patrick (R) denounced the resolution stating, "I will not stand by and let looney Marxist UT professors poison the minds of young students with critical race Theory. We banned it in publicly funded K-12, and we will ban it in publicly funded higher ed."[30] According to Patrick and his Republican Party allies, teaching about social justice amounts to a Marxist plot threatening Western civilization.

This stuff is hard to make up, but given its emergence and dangerous consequences in the 1950s, dominated by an anti-communist hysteria, it cannot be ignored.[31]

Donald Trump went further when he invoked the rhetoric of the McCarthy era at a rally in Florence, North Carolina, on March 12, 2022. He told his followers that they should be willing to "lay down their very lives" to defend America against critical race theory. As Trump put it:

> The fate of any nation depends upon the willingness of its citizens to lay down – and they must do this – lay down their very lives to defend their country. If we allow the Marxists and communists and socialists to teach our children to hate America there will be no one left to defend our flag or to protect our great country or its freedom.[32]

In this instance, Trump urges his followers to resist the teaching of critical race theory, which is not taught in public schools, and endorses a language supporting violence in the service of a race war is what an updated version of fascism looks like.

Elements of censorship, repression, and an authoritarian culture also become clear in the shameless propaganda produced by right-wing foundations, anti-public intellectual media pundits, and politicians who embrace the "big lie" and the ongoing politics of censorship and book burning. This depoliticizing culture operates through multiple technologies, screen cultures, and video games that trade endlessly in images of violence, spectacles of consumption, and stultifying modes of manufactured ignorance. Civic literacy has morphed into a form of civic illiteracy as matters of truth, evidence, and rationality give way to a culture based on misinformation, a hatred of dissent, an embrace of a dangerous anti-intellectualism, and support for a number of bizarre conspiracy theories. Rather than push at the frontiers of the imagination, education in the broadest sense now promotes forms of ignorance, conformity, and modes of organized irresponsibility. With the collapse of those ideologies and modes of civic literacy that offer a sense of political agency, individual autonomy, and the ability to think critically, there is the further collapse of the democratic public spheres that make them possible.

Funded by right-wing ideological, corporate, and militaristic interests, an army of anti-public intellectuals groomed in right-wing think tanks and foundations dominates the traditional media, polices the universities for any vestige of critical thought and dissent, and endlessly spreads their message of privatization, deregulation, and commercialization, exercising a powerful influence in the dismantling of all public spheres not dominated by private and commodifying interests. These "experts in legitimation," to use Antonio Gramsci's prescient phrase, peddle civic ignorance just as they renounce any vestige of public accountability for an army of Trump lackeys, giant media conglomerates, massive propaganda machines, and financial elites.

Neoliberalism's quest for short-term profits, investments, and enrichment has suppressed the price and social costs paid for the mass-produced short-term attention spans, 24-hour inundations of game and reality TV shows, and the relentless illiteracy reproduced via the worship of celebrity culture. Life behind the illusions, imitations, and simulacra is buried in the lies, the quest for immediate pleasure, and the search for instant gratification. It has become more difficult for people to escape from the ideological terror machinery of a culture that convinces them that all their problems are a matter of individual responsibility, that matters of class, racism, misogyny, and other forms of oppression are individual rather than systemic problems, and that the privatization of everything legitimates collapsing the political into the therapeutic language of the personal. The forces of depoliticization annihilate any viable notion of politics and collective resistance while also creating the conditions that make it easier for the United States to move to a full-fledged, refurbished fascist social order. Lost here is the crucial insight that there is no genuine democracy, collective move for resistance, and defense of public goods without genuine opposing critical power, and that such power is at its core educational.

The failure of the progressives to acknowledge this is evident in too many short-sighted treatments of the Republican Party's attack on critical race theory, progressive books, and critical forms of pedagogy.

This is not simply an attack on history as dangerous memory, dissent, academic freedom, and racial injustice. This is a much broader attack on the very institutions that produce engaged citizens, critical agency, and critical thought itself. It is code for preventing students from learning how to make informed judgments, engage the arguments of others, marshal evidence, and communicate bravely and with clarity—skills essential to assuming the role of a citizen. The attack on critical race theory is a full-fledged assault on both the democratizing purpose of education and the institutions that support its democratic possibilities.[33] Under the narrow rubric of an attack on critical race theory, we are witnessing a wider assault on the ability to link moral authority with intellectual competencies. These attacks also undermine the ability to learn from history and engage civic virtues in order to address the most malign threats to social and economic justice.

At the core of this attack on education is an attempt to fashion pedagogies of repression in which students are not taught to think analytically, weigh evidence, consider different points of view, and distinguish between historical misinformation and historical reality. One consequence will be students unable to discuss the critical issues of the day, distinguish fact from fantasy, and learn from history. One outcome of this repressive view of school is creating a generation of "adults who are prey to the self-serving and inaccurate claims of demagogic leaders."[34]

The war against the culture of critique, accountability, dissent, reason, justice, and critical agency has moved into full throttle with the current attacks on language and meaning. In the current era of authoritarianism, meaning as a form of truth-telling is stripped out of language. Truth is no longer discernible from lies, and terrorism takes the form of eliminating the thinking subject, the common good, and all forms of meaningful solidarity. In other words, the casualties of authoritarianism include the minds that oppose it.

As such, the current attacks on critical race theory become an excuse for attacking all institutions where students and others might realize themselves as critical citizens. Judd Legum provides a telling instance of the latter in his critical analyses of how right-wing extremists are waging war against public education in Tennessee. The attacks on issues dealing with racism and social justice are being conducted through both repressive pedagogical practices and threats to ban "instructional material that include ... poorly defined concepts" such as 'privilege,' "discomfort," and other terms that reinsure that the language of erasure works to mis-educate students while imposing a form of historical amnesia.[35] This is a form of violence that cripples language, elevates stupidity over reason, and disregards the truth in order to promote lies and conspiracy theories. It is a machinery of annihilation that connects the power of corporate wealth and religious fanaticism to a politics of racial cleansing and the degradation of civic literacy, civic courage, and civic culture. Rather than put an end to history, it simply makes it unrecognizable.

Reclaiming the past and connecting it to the present is not only a political act but also a civic necessity. The danger of not doing so legitimates the authoritarian impulse to "reshape the historical record, removing evidence of past persecutions to make it easier for people to engage in new discriminations and violence."[36] Legum provides an example of this authoritarian strategy in his claim that the dark money-funded group Moms for Liberty is waging a war of censorship against any book that includes social justice issues, and has gone so far as to object to including such highly celebrated books as *Martin Luther King, Jr., and the March on Washington*. One criticism of the book made by Moms for Liberty was that it displayed "photographs of white firemen blasting black children to the point of 'bruising their bodies and ripping off their clothes'."[37] Legum also points out in a forceful example that the group "objected to the teacher's manual accompanying the book because it had a negative depiction of Bull Connor, the notorious racist who used hoses and attack dogs to enforce segregation."[38]

It is worth noting that Robin Steenman, the head of Williamson County chapter of Moms for Liberty, once stated on her Twitter account, which has since been deleted, that "she would never send her kids to a public school and described public school teachers as 'brainwashing assholes'."[39] It gets worse. The Moms for Liberty movement not only engages in whitewashing of history for public school children but also tries to impose their own white supremacist version of history. For example, their website recommends that students learn about American history through the lens of *The Making of America*, a book published in 1985 by W. Cleon Skousen, who died in 2006. According to Legum,

Skousen was a supporter of The John Birch Society, a far-right organization that opposed the civil rights movement ... Skousen's book characterizes "Black children as 'pickaninnies' and American slave owners as the 'worst victims' of slavery."

The book claims that the Founders wished to free the slaves but "[m]ost of [the slaves] were woefully unprepared for a life of competitive independence." Skousen asserts that abolitionists "did much to perpetuate slavery" by taking a "too militant" approach.[40]

Moms for Liberty has also been highly influential in promoting legislation that includes mandatory punishment for teachers and librarians who resist censorship policies. One egregious example of such legislation pending in Oklahoma "gives parents the right to object to any book in a public school library. If that book isn't removed within 30 days, the librarian must be fired and cannot be rehired for two years, and the complainant is eligible for $10,000 a day in damages until the book is removed."[41] Moms for Liberty has gone so far as to put "a $500 bounty on the heads of teachers for addressing issues about race and equity in their classrooms deemed inappropriate by a New Hampshire gag order."[42] This reactionary white supremacist pedagogy aimed at destroying public and higher education and the promise of a multiracial democracy must be held accountable through forms of schooling and popular education that do more than promote an anti-racist consciousness; it must also be addressed by first recognizing that underlying this fascist politics is a crisis of consciousness that, as Angela Davis points out, must be challenged through educational practices that adopt "a critical stance in which people can perceive their relationship to reality."[43]

At the heart of such a struggle is the question of what is the purpose of education? What role should it play in a democracy? More specifically, what does it mean to address education in a time of tyranny? We might ask ourselves how critical pedagogy can live up to its democratic principles by addressing the forces of white supremacy, racism, class differences, and patriarchy.[44] How might education become central to politics and take on the goal of educating students and the public to think critically and learn how to challenge the perpetrators of white supremacy and social violence? Moreover, it is crucial to not only defend education against authoritarian forces, particularly in the Republican Party and right-wing conservative foundations, but also to rethink what think tanks and progressive foundations need to be developed and sustained for a multiracial democracy to be defended and sustained in such dark times.

A radical politics cannot survive if it ignores or downplays the fact that public and higher education are one of the few spheres left in democratic societies where students and others can learn the knowledge and skills of democratic citizenship. Nor can it survive if it ignores the powerful role of education outside of schools in a massive ecosystem of high-tech driven, digital cultural apparatuses that serve as steering mechanisms that package ideas, domesticate radical ideas, and narrow public discourse. At the same time, it is not the job of education to confuse education with training, nor is its job only to educate students for the workforce or impose a regime of repressive conformity on teachers and students and the wider public. Moreover, the job of education is not to build "human capital" and reduce the obligations of citizenship to the demands of consumerism and corporate capital, but to educate young people and others to address the most important problems of the day, extending from climate change and systemic racism to the threat of nuclear war.

CHAPTER THIRTEEN

Politics under Siege

The left and progressives need a new language for connecting politics, power, culture, and everyday life. This should be a language that embraces the power of pedagogy, beliefs, and persuasion as central political tools. With the rise of image-based politics, new technologically driven forms of social media, and more threatening and complicated relations of power, there is a need for new theories, visions, and modes of resistance capable of changing the current authoritarian threats to democracy. It is important to stress once again that central to such a language is the recognition that education is central to politics because it is about changing the way people think, see things, and identify with narratives that enable them to become both critical and engaged agents. This suggests viewing cultural institutions such as schools, mainstream and alternative media such as print and audio culture, diverse entertainment platforms, and social media as vital sites of political and pedagogical struggle.

There is a need to rethink and re-examine the radical treatment of culture and education that emerged in the 1970s and 1980s in the fields of cultural studies, media studies, and the sociology of education. This proposes building on the work of theorists such as Antonio Gramsci, Raymond Williams, Paulo Freire, Angela Davis, Audre Lord, Adrienne Rich, bell hooks, and others, including Frederick Jameson, Stuart Hall, Larry Grossberg, Ellen Willis, and Stanley Aronowitz, whose work has greatly enriched our understanding of cultural politics and critical education. As Cornelius Castoriadis, John Dewey, and W. B. DuBois have argued in different terms, "people need to be educated for democracy by not only expanding the capacities that enable them to assume public responsibility but also through active participation in the very process of governing."[1]

If a form of democratic resistance is to take place to avoid a fascist coup in the future, it is essential to develop a new language for equating freedom and democracy, challenging the basic tenets of neoliberal capitalism, and aligning the push for civic literacy with the development of a political building strategy whose purpose is to infuse and energize the struggle for a unified left-party dedicated to the principles of democratic socialism.[2] Real substantive and lasting change will not come without a mass-based movement in America. Angela Davis has long advocated that a multigenerational racial and mass-based working-class movement, coupled with a radical shift in consciousness about what kind of world we want to live in, is the key to radical change. She is worth quoting at length:

> what I am saying is that in order to make real, lasting change, we have to do the work of building movements. It is masses of people who are responsible for historical change. It was because of the movement, the Black freedom movement, the midcentury Black freedom movement, that Black people acquired the right to vote—not because someone decided to pass a Voting Rights Act. And we know now that that victory cannot simply be consolidated as a bill passed, because there are continual efforts to suppress the power of Black voters. And we know that the only way to reverse that is by building movements, by involving masses of people in the process of historical change. And this holds true for the current administration.[3]

While the emergence of a mass political movement is essential to challenging neoliberal capitalism, it is imperative to mobilize diverse working-class elements as part of this struggle. This is especially true given that labor is once again pushing back against capitalism. We live at a moment when gangster capitalism with its highly concentrated financial and corporate power has become more savage, creating the conditions where it can no longer seduce the working-class with the promise of more consumer goods, full employment, social mobility, and the fake appeal to individual responsibility.

Neoliberalism's disimagination machines function through a discourse of denial and repression. As a mode of denial, it attempts to make the dangerous memories of history and existing inequalities disappear. In doing so, it refuses to acknowledge the subjugated knowledges that can lay claim to alternative histories.[4] As a mode of repression, it produces modes of agency in which individuals are defined as isolated automatons. In addition, neoliberalism's pedagogical efforts at individualizing social problems and convincing people to retreat into the privatized space of the self is matched at the policy level by the production of extreme and cruel austerity measures coupled with the relentless commercialization of social relations.

As part of capitalism's fantasy structure, it celebrates the self-made human being, separates economic activity from social costs, rejects the social contract, and radicalizes a regressive notion of individual responsibility that eliminates ethical assessments and the grammar of social responsibility. One consequence is that neoliberal material entanglements of power are less visible and have been successful in undermining public values while creating a sense of deep despair, alienation, and loneliness in the public imagination. The privatized self so central to neoliberal notions of agency increases fear and loneliness, and tears up social solidarities.

This "fixed hedonism," as Žižek calls it, has become the ruling ideology of the day.[5] Hannah Arendt goes further and argues that terror rules over people when they are isolated and deem themselves powerless, and convinces them that they can no longer engage the conditions that suppress them. She believed that totalitarianism destroyed "the public realm of life ... by isolating men [and] their political capacities."[6] When people no longer belong to the world, they experience not only loneliness but a distrust of others. Under such circumstances, civic culture wanes, public spheres whither, and politics appears hopeless. In her discussion of Arendt and totalitarianism, Anne Applebaum captures how this redefined notion of terror destroyed civic life and magnified a toxic isolation that undermined both resistance and politics itself. She writes:

> By destroying civic institutions, whether sports clubs or small businesses, totalitarian regimes kept people away from one another and prevented them from sharing creative or productive projects. By blanketing the public sphere with propaganda, they

made people afraid to speak with one another. And when each person felt himself isolated from the rest, resistance became impossible. Politics in the broadest sense became impossible. ... In a world where everyone is supposedly 'connected,' loneliness and isolation once again are smothering activism, optimism, and the desire to participate in public life.[7]

With the death of the social, isolation and loneliness have created an updated form of terror, preparing the conditions for totalitarianism. Neoliberalism enacts a public pedagogy that destroys trust, isolates individuals, and depoliticizes them by claiming that harsh competition should replace the public good and that all forms of solidarity when not driven by market values are a sign of weakness. In this scenario, everyone is trapped in their own feelings, a privatized space blinded by an unchecked belief in untethered self-reliance and self-interest. Matters of health, sickness, poverty, joblessness, and homelessness, among other troubles, are reduced "to individual limitations, faulty character, or moral failures rather than as symptoms of a sick society."[8] In the world of corporate mindfulness and therapy, the politics of depoliticization is on full display as social problems collapse into the discourse of self-help.[9] As John Steppling observes, "in a therapy culture adjustment and adaptation are the prevailing rules of life."[10] Public goods, values, and investments are now subordinated to the quest for profits and the enshrinement of private interests.

Hermetically sealed from any sense of social responsibility and defined through a mounting egoism and self-centeredness, individuals run the risk of slipping into a kind of ethical somnolence, indifferent to the plight and suffering of others, while bearing the burden of being told that whatever problems they face they have no one to blame but themselves. Judith Butler's concept of "a sociality that exceeds" atomized individuals gives way to a ruthless Hobbesian world where all activity, but especially economic activity, is removed from social costs.[11] Neoliberalism's unchecked logic of self-reliance and personal responsibility celebrates a pathological disdain for community, tears up social solidarities, tells people they have to navigate life alone, and in doing so, creates a culture of cruelty and a political and corporate reign of monsters. Neoliberalism does more than devalue human life; it empties politics of its democratic values and pressures, disparages democratic visions, closes down political horizons, views emancipated notions of solidarity and mass struggle with contempt, and reinforces these actions by way of producing repressive modes of education in its vast complex of disimagination machines.

The demagogues created in the undercurrents of neoliberalism inhabit an illiberal vision of the world and seethe with what Applebaum claims is the "language of resentment, aggression, and imperial nostalgia."[12] She is right in arguing that "unless democracies defend themselves together, the forces of autocracy will destroy them."[13] What she misses is the role that education and public pedagogy have played in producing a public that supports this wave of authoritarianism, and the equally important role it has to play in creating a public consciousness and social imagination as a bulwark against fascism. She suggests that Americans need to "Take democracy seriously. Teach it, debate it, improve it, defend it."[14] Sounds good, but without a theoretical and rigorous understanding of how central education is to politics and how it works both in the schools and in wider cultural apparatuses, her suggestion falls into the category of a feel-good, easy-to-quote slogan.

CHAPTER FOURTEEN

The Necessity of a Comprehensive Politics

The left and other progressives need to create a counter-revolution in values and a system of meaning capable of addressing the cultural forces shaping policies, dominant ideas, and broader social forces. Moreover, this struggle must work to bring together the wide range of movements fighting for emancipation, social equality, ecological, sexual, racial, and economic justice. Movements for social justice are too fractured, rooted in silos that often fail to address the shared roots of oppression at work under neoliberal capitalism and an expanding fascist politics. Of course, there are exceptions. Some modern left movements have performed a vital theoretical and political service in highlighting diverse forms of oppression and the heightened needs of society's disadvantage. These include movements extending from the Black Lives Matter movement, #MeToo to Fight for $15, and Extinction Rebellion, among others, which have made visible the continuing problems of racial profiling, police violence, ecological destruction, economic inequality, the carceral state, and the widespread assaults waged on women.

The authors of *Abolition. Feminism. Now* provide one important example of a much needed relational and comprehensive politics. For instance, they are quite clear when talking about prison reform. They argue that the conversation cannot be limited to simply Black people and must include "immigration detention, Indigenous incarceration" and "other kinds of factors that make incarceration a problem."[1] Moreover, they argue that the problem of mass incarceration cannot be restricted to the brutalizing institutions of the punishing state. Broader considerations such as neoliberalism, massive inequality, poverty, systemic racism, and oppressive forms of education, among others, must also come into play. Only then does the full scope of the carceral state become visible in both its specificity and the broader context in which it functions.

To effectively challenge gangster capitalism and the rising forces of white supremacy, isolated social movements will need to connect with other movements by broadening their appeals to a range of disadvantaged groups while addressing wider social problems and forms of oppression.[2] For instance, it is crucial to integrate class and racial struggles as central categories in the development of mass movements. In part, this also means moving beyond the language of critique by proposing policies that appeal to a broad coalition— policies that speak to people's needs and offer the promise of building lasting institutions. Political capital can be gained by forging alliances among working-class communities that include people of color and speak to the ways in which various forms of inequality bear down on their lives.[3] Doing so offers the possibility of connecting their diverse struggles to an expansive and generalized notion of justice and equality.[4] This is especially significant at a time when Americans have lost the ability to connect the dots between their personal anxieties, fears, and uncertainties and larger political events and systemic forces.

Sam Gindin offers another take on the need for a radical mass movement organized around the working class. He states that "the revival of the working-class as a social force is the definitive economic and political challenge now confronting the American left."[5] The good news is that the energy around unionizing seems to be growing. The key to such strikes is both the reduction of the power of corporations and an increase in the power of workers.[6] The latter cannot take place without a mass worker movement. Moreover, such a movement cannot develop without first educating workers through left cultural apparatuses that make corporate power visible and offer diverse platforms for workers and others to raise their class consciousness, develop strategic skills and confidence, and recommend possibilities for the broadest membership participation. Clearly, this cannot happen if workers remain isolated in their individual unions and narrowly defined political and economic struggles. Gindin spells out the rubrics of such a challenge. He writes:

> The challenge—the active organizing challenge—is to build on the contradictions within capitalism to support the remaking of the working-class: to develop the individual and collective potentials of workers into a coherent, confident, and creative social force capable of leading a struggle against not only their employer but eventually capitalism itself.[7]

Across the United States, workers are striking, attempting to unionize, or both. This is a daunting challenge given that less than 11 percent of the entire working class belong to a union. Hope lies in the fact that a new surge of labor resistance is evident in strikes and organizing attempts at Kroger, Starbucks, John Deere, Amazon, Apple, and Uber, among other sites. Union victories in 2022 at Amazon and Starbucks suggest that because of the changing labor landscape due to the pandemic, which highlighted workplace safety and harsh working conditions among other issues, new opportunities have opened up for unions.[8]

Other examples include a rash of teacher strikes, as unions exercise once again their power of collective resistance.[9] For instance, on March 8, 2022, the Minneapolis Federation of Teachers went on strike after enduring years of austerity measures that were as onerous as they were cruel. Plagued by large classes, meager salaries, lack of teacher diversity, and a shortage of essential resources, teachers were treated as disposable, second-class citizens. One high school teacher, Ma-Riah Roberson-Moody, reports that she makes a paltry $24,000 a year, and has to work other jobs in order to care for her family. In an interview with *NBC News* she stated "I'm fighting to stay at this job because I really, really love what I'm doing. But I just do not make enough money. I can make more money right now going to work at Target than I do working for Minneapolis Public Schools, and that is difficult."[10]

It is not surprising that so many teachers in the United States need a second job to make ends meet. In fact, "nearly 1 in 5 American public-school teachers work a second job outside of the classroom";[11] too many hold third jobs and work on the weekend. Too many teachers suffer from what is termed a "wage penalty"; "that is they make less money on the dollar than their peers in comparable fields" even when they hold doctoral degrees.[12] Wage slavery is the more appropriate term for this abuse of our nation's teachers. Fortunately, many teachers across the United States are fighting back against this frontal assault on public education.[13] At the heart of this war on teachers is a war on public schools, not because they are failing but because they are public and are essential in any democracy that lives or dies by the degree to which its citizens are well educated.

This surge of worker resistance suggests that mass politics should be on the agenda for social change and that matters of class and racial justice must be central to such a mass-based movement. One example of such worker resistance took place when Walt Disney Company's LGBT+ employees and company workers staged walk outs in response to Disney's halfhearted response to Florida's "Don't Say Gay" legislation. The workers were not striking over traditional wage and labor issues. Instead, they wanted Disney, the largest employer, to condemn "the anti-LGBT+ legislation and stop funding Republican legislators and state officials who supported the bill."[14] The protests forced Disney CEO Bob Chapek to apologize for an earlier response and pledge to take opposition to the bill more seriously. The Disney protest movement once again made clear that it is crucial that mass resistance happen through struggles that address not only workplace issues but also issues fundamental to "a more egalitarian, democratic, environmentally sustainable society."[15]

One caveat. As admirable as this strike was, it must be acknowledged that what is necessary for a revival of unions in America is a strong working-class movement that also attacks widening inequality, the erosion of labor standards, systemic racism, and liberal attempts to integrate unions into corporate-controlled bureaucratic workplace structures.[16] What needs to be addressed in any movement for mass resistance is the role of education and cultural politics in shaping individual and social agency while still recognizing the inequalities imposed by the materiality of power.

A new political vision is needed, in which class struggle is both refined and integrated with anti-racist movements and larger issues of culture and education. Most important is the need to recognize that racial justice cannot be separated from economic justice, nor from the cultural politics that inform these issues.[17] Neither movement can be removed entirely from the other and must be viewed once again as central conceptual and political forces fundamental to building a mass multiracial movement. The brilliant historian Robin D. G. Kelley is on target in stating that the United States needs a multiracial labor movement committed to "dismantling the oppressive regimes of racism, heteropatriarchy, empire, and class exploitation that is at the root of inequality, precarity, materialism and violence in many forms."[18] Moreover, collective resistance must be defined by a radically democratic project intent on overthrowing capitalism, which is a radical evil, source of malignant injustice, and force for untold suffering. Reform cannot be confused with a revolutionary project.

The building of mass-based social movements should be guided by a political imagination intent on moving beyond demonstrations, which are useful pedagogical events, to the long-term task of coordinating and sustaining alternative institutions that extend from worker-controlled workplaces to alternative media outlets and educational spaces. Central to such change is the necessity to launch an educational campaign that makes clear how neoliberal capitalism has sowed the seeds of fascism not only in the United States but also across the globe. Consequently, mass consciousness becomes foundational in inspiring, educating, energizing, and organizing such a mass political movement.

Progressives have to develop a more comprehensive view of oppression and political struggle. This is a lesson that Martin Luther King Jr. understood all too well in his call for the need to radically restructure American society by drawing connections between racism, militarism, and capitalism.[19] What is to be learned in the current historical moment is that the struggle against racism, class exploitation, and sexism cannot be removed from struggles for eliminating student debt, economic justice, the financialization of social existence, mass impoverishment, abolition of the carceral state, and ecological rights.

One major challenge in developing this struggle would be to carve out a protective and safe space for those working-class communities whose members are burdened by the demands of surviving. Informal networks, associations, community services, and educational spaces have to be developed that allow people not to be trapped by the burden of time, unable to participate in the privilege of being politically active.

This strategy suggests a politics that takes up the challenge of workable alliances. It also states that more concentrated attention be given both to institutional changes and to changes regarding matters of subjectivity, consciousness, identity, and cultural politics. Central to such a project is the need to build a mass-based movement in which different progressive groups can unite under the banner of struggling together for economic, racial, and social justice, all of which are vital for developing an argument for a radical socialist democracy. In this case, the struggle over power relations would involve not only challenging economic institutions and other dominant structures of domination but would also include an ongoing project to wage a struggle through diverse forms of political education on the terrain of popular culture. In this way, education would, once again, be central to any movement for resistance and social change. This call for an intersectional politics is necessary for not only rethinking the future but also rethinking politics itself.

Developing a politics of the totality, one that allows people to understand the interconnections among the various social justice struggles, enables individuals to gain a broader understanding of how diverse issues such as race, class, and gender are integrated and reinforce each other—a task essential to developing an effective politics of resistance necessitates conceiving of neoliberal capitalism and its fascist politics as a single integrated set of relations. A politics of totality should provide a historical and relational language—one that illuminates how institutions, culture, and habits arise within specific social relations. This is a language that rejects master narratives for formative narratives.

Under such circumstances, as Angela Davis has long argued, gender, for instance, cannot be considered aside from class and race. In addition, there is also the necessity for developing a discourse of possibility as fundamental to imagining a radical notion of social change. As Theodor Adorno once put it, "a utopianism that is the transformation of the totality, and the imagination of such a transformation of the totality is basically very different [than] a very modest, very narrow" view of change.[20] What complicates this view is that viable change has to come from below, and the best hope for this is among young people, especially those who have been left out of the script of democracy. The signposts for such change are all around us, but for it to happen, it will take a massive educational and political effort to mobilize such resistance.

As I mention in this book, political education and cultural politics are essential for individuals to learn how diverse struggles have worked together in the past, and what they can teach us about promoting a shift in popular consciousness at a moment of tyranny, crisis, and mass anxiety. Dominant political, pedagogical, and cultural forces in the current moment weigh heavily against the possibility or dream of change, making the terrain of subjectivity and consciousness all the more vital an arena of struggle. Joao Biehl is right in stating that "subjectivity is the material of politics,"[21] while suggesting the question of how, for instance, popular education and radical art can be used to promote an anti-capitalist consciousness in order to re-imagine a just and dignified economic, political, and social future.[22]

PART FOUR

Towards an Insurrectional Democracy

CHAPTER FIFTEEN

Hideous Freedoms: Lessons to be Learned from the Convoy Movement

The concept of freedom must be rescued from the individualizing project of neoliberal ideology and its revamped notion of fascist politics, which has reduced the meaning of freedom to the spheres of self-interest, the personal, and a regressive notion of consumption. Under neoliberalism, freedom removes agency from any talk about social responsibility. This radical individualization of responsibility constructs an atomized, self-absorbed notion of agency trapped in an utterly privatized and competitive conception of the self. This is a self in which compassion and care for the other disappear, as do the social forms and protections that make human bonds possible. It is a view of the self and freedom unmoored from any notion of solidarity connected to a viable notion of the social contract and the social imagination.

This regressive notion of freedom is no longer limited to the realm of philosophy; it has become a driving ideological and political force among the emerging right-wing in the United States. For instance, David Frum argues that the most egregious displays of freedom in the name of violence now function for many of Trump's followers "as a statement of identity and a test of loyalty."[1] Removed from the discourse of the common good, equality, and social rights, individual freedom now aligns with the mob—positioning itself with those willing in the age of the pandemic to sacrifice other people's lives in the name of a bogus appeal to personal rights.

This abuse of freedom is not limited to the United States. In Canada, the "Freedom Convoy" movement that took place in February 2022 consisted of hundreds of trucks that ground to a halt at the busiest border crossing between Canada and the United States. The convoy also occupied Ottawa, Canada's capital, effectively blockading the city and disrupting daily life for most residents in its core. Before the Canadian police cleared the Ambassador Bridge between Detroit and Windsor, which the protest brought to a halt, the Freedom movement inflicted serious economic damage, especially in the auto industries on both sides of the border. Some estimates indicated that the costs of disrupting US supply chains and international trade amounted to over $300 million a day. The convoy participants rejected all vaccine requirements and mandates and supported a decidedly anti-government discourse reminiscent of far-right ideology in the United States. As *New York Times* writer Paul Krugman observes, "beyond rejecting health measures intended to save lives," the protest movement is really "an attempt to exploit pandemic weariness to boost the usual culture-war agenda."[2] The convoy participants lacked the support of the Canadian general public, which is largely vaccinated. In Ottawa, residents in one neighborhood "confronted and disrupted several truckers who were on their way downtown to join the so-called 'Freedom Convoy'."[3]

The residents forced the truck drivers to remove signs, flags, and stickers on their trucks supporting far-right slogans and had them "surrender their jerry cans, making it more difficult for them to refuel once they reached downtown."[4] The convoy also lacked the backing not only of most Canadian truckers, 90 percent of whom were vaccinated, but also the Canadian Trucking Alliance (CTA). The powerful Teamsters Union, with members in both the United States and Canada, denounced the "Freedom Convoy."[5] After days of inaction, Prime Minister Trudeau invoked the Emergencies Act for the first time in Canadian history and declared a public emergency. As a response to ending the protests and blockades, the act gave the federal government wide-sweeping power.[6] Soon afterward, the major disruptive protests in Canada came to an end.

The truckers had been primarily endorsed by leading far-right US Republicans such as Donald Trump, Ted Cruz, Rand Paul, Marjorie

Taylor Greene, and some Canadian conservative politicians. Support also came from powerful anti-democratic social media figures such as Tucker Carlson, Jordan Peterson, Sean Hannity, Elon Musk, and many white supremacist groups.[7] True to his deeply authoritarian politics, Elon Musk went so far as to compare the Canadian prime minister, Justin Trudeau, to Adolf Hitler.[8]

The irony here is hard to miss. These same American politicians and right-wing stooges were quick to denounce earlier demonstrations by the Black Lives Movement against police violence and systemic racism as an "orgy of violence." By contrast, they supported the right-wing inspired convoy protests regardless of the latter becoming a flashpoint for a range of white supremacist and neo-Nazi groups. One harsh critic of the BLM, Senator Rand Paul, stated that "I hope the truckers do come to America, and I hope they clog up cities."[9] This is an odd call for lawlessness coming from someone who, like his Republican Party colleagues, has made a career endorsing what amounts to a national frenzy posturing for "law and order," especially evident in his once racist rhetoric denouncing Black Lives Matter demonstrators as a "crazed mob."[10]

Some of Canada's more powerful right-wing groups backing the "Freedom Convoy" included Action4Canada. The latter group made the false and conspiracy-riddled claims that the COVID-19 pandemic "was carried out, at least in part, by Bill Gates and a 'New World (Economic) Order' to facilitate the injection of 5G-enabled microchips into the population."[11] As Professor Stephanie Carvin, a specialist in international law, security terrorism, and technology, observed, this movement brought "together extremists, religious movements, fringe politicians, and the far-right media."[12] Furthermore, she writes that social media played a powerful role in giving people both a cause and a sense of connection and "belonging, at a time when we've been forced to be separated ... These people feel like they're part of something far beyond themselves. And they're live streaming 24/7."[13]

The "Freedom Convoy" protests were the brainchild of James Bauder, who heads the Canada Unity movement, which launched the protests. Bauder believes in baseless conspiracy theories and "has endorsed the QAnon movement and called Covid-19 'the biggest political scam in history'."[14] Bauder is no friend of organized labor and, as *Jacobin* has noted, in 2020 he participated in another convoy called United We Roll that "planned an anti-union protest where convoy members threatened to dismantle the picket line and run over workers."[15]

Other leaders in the movement include some hard-right extremists, such as Patrick King, who once "stated that he believes the vaccine was created to 'depopulate' the white race."[16] Another convoy leader, B. J. Dichter, has a reputation for spreading Islamophobic sentiments.[17] The Canadian Anti-Hate Network, a non-profit group, has reported that "The so-called 'Freedom Convoy' was organized by known far-right figures who have espoused Islamophobic, anti-Semitic and other hateful views."[18]

For example, the Ottawa protests made crystal clear that extreme elements supporting fascism and white nationalism were attracted to the movement, and this was visible in the appearance of neo-Nazi and Confederate flags and an abundance of QAnon logos emblazoned on trucks, signs, and stickers. Moreover, some sources noted that a significant amount of funding, over $8 million as of February 7, 2022, had come from right-wing sources in the United States.[19] *The Washington Post* reported that 42 percent of the money raised by the combined fundraising platforms GiveSendGo, Freedom Convoy 2022, and Adopt-a-Trucker came from the United States.[20] Some of the largest individual donations have come from American billionaires.[21] Funding from the States has so alarmed members of the Canadian New Democratic Party that they have called it "an attack on Canada's democracy" and have asked the US ambassador "to testify before the House of Commons foreign affairs committee."[22]

Jagmeet Singh, the leader of the NDP, stated that what happened in Ottawa was more than a protest movement. On the contrary, he argued that the convoy's stated intent is to "overthrow the government."[23] The convoy association "with hate groups ... expressing racist and anti-immigrant sentiments ... could explain why the 'Freedom Convoy' is strangely silent on labor issues facing immigrant truckers who now make up over one-third of truckers in Canada," writes Emily Leedham in *Jacobin*.[24] She further notes "that many of the concerns of the protesters have little to do with workers' rights or labor issues within Canada's trucking industry. In fact, convoy organizers have previously harassed workers on the picket line and ignored calls for support from racialized truckers fighting against wage theft."[25]

Freedom was, once again, hijacked in the interest of a counter-revolution whose purpose was to destroy the authority of the government to protect the common good, limit the influence of the financial and corporate elite, and protect civic structures critical to a democracy. The Ottawa truckers motivated right-wing convoy movements across the globe, and their growing influence made it clear that they were winning the global information war.[26]

Elisabeth R. Anker argues that the right-wing in the United States is increasingly using the language of "ugly freedoms" to promote an "anti-democratic politics [that] threatens to overtake freedom's meaning entirely, harnessing freedom solely to projects of exclusion, privilege and harm."[27] She writes:

'Ugly freedoms' are used to block the teaching of certain ideas, diminish employees' ability to have power in the workplace and undermine public health. These are not merely misunderstood freedoms, or even just a cynical use of the language of freedom to frame bigoted policies. They manifest, instead, a particular interpretation of freedom that is not expansive, but exclusionary and coercive.[28]

This notion of "ugly freedom" is certainly applicable to the convoy movement and much of the anti-vaccine protests in the United States. Lost in its neoliberal view of freedom is any notion of an "inclusive freedom" that contests authoritarian and anti-democratic modes of suppression such as the concentration of wealth and power in the hands of a financial elite, the rise of the punishing state, mass poverty, the rise of war culture, ecological devastation, and the criminalization of social problems such as homelessness. Both Canadian convoy protesters and those in the United States have been silent regarding the notion of inclusive freedom—one that would argue for universal health care, expanding workers' unions, introducing regulations that ensure worker safety and paid sick days, and the need for social and wage benefits for unemployed workers.

Under this form of gangster capitalism, freedom is hollowed out, removed from any sense of social solidarity, forcing individuals to bear full responsibility for the problems they confront even though they are not of their own making. As Zygmunt Bauman rightly observes, existential insecurity is intensified as individuals are now "left to find and practice individual solutions to socially produced troubles ... while being equipped with tools and resources that are blatantly inadequate to the task."[29]

The dangers of unchecked individualism cannot be separated from struggles over democracy, especially when freedom becomes a rationale for undermining human dependency, the common good, and support for mutual solidarity. When wedded to neoliberal notions of individualism, the call to freedom weakens human bonds and makes solidarity difficult to recognize and practice. This danger has become apparent as the appeal to freedom is used to resist COVID-19 vaccination efforts and mask mandates—a tactic that is code for an allegiance to the political right.[30] Vaccine scientist Peter Hotez adds to this position, arguing that for the most part, the anti-vax, freedom-at-all-cost movement engages in "anti-science aggression" and "is a component of authoritarian rule [cultivated by] their own cadre of pseudo intellectuals."[31] Hotez makes clear that the appeal to freedom to buttress an anti-vax, anti-science movement has degenerated into a "killing force."[32] One can clearly apply this analysis to the convoy movement that has emerged across the globe.

What Hotez and other critics of the anti-vax movement, including the convoy protests, miss is how neoliberalism remakes the social into the biographical, further convincing individuals that they have no obligation to contribute to health, safety, and democratic institutions that shape the wider community. Too many Americans consign to oblivion the relationship between liberty and the greater good. This is on full display given the self-righteous, if not violent, behavior that is often waged in the name of freedom by Trump's supporters.[33] In a society where civic culture and civic education are under siege, self-interests align with narrow market values, and the truth is derided, freedom loses its meaning and increasingly becomes a term that justifies demagogic values and practices. The far-right populist movements emerging in the United States and abroad represent an attack on public health and science, and point to something other than a struggle over freedom; they are part of a larger authoritarian movement to destroy democracy in the name of freedom.

In a hyper-driven market society such as the United States, freedom is largely defined as the freedom from, including freedom from government constraints and freedom from acting on one's self-interests.[34] What is missing in this discourse, banished from neoliberal ideology, is the freedom to struggle to expand the conditions for agency and a life of dignity by eliminating economic, racial, and gender inequalities. The 2022 Oxfam report titled "*Inequality Kills*" makes clear that massive inequality in all areas of life produces forms of economic violence that destroy lives, undermine politics, and put the ecological life of the planet at risk.[35]

United by the call to make education a fundamental part of politics, progressives must work to create the institutions and public spheres in which democracy is understood in the first instance as the sharing of power among everyone, not a financial elite. Freedom has to be articulated as the ability for individuals to experience themselves as critically engaged citizens "who experience their fate collectively and are willing to act on it together."[36] Erich Fromm was right in stating that a democratic notion of freedom "stands for freedom from fear, want, oppression, and violence. But freedom is not only from but also freedom to; freedom to participate actively and responsibly in all decisions concerning the citizen, freedom to develop the individual's human potential to the fullest possible degree."[37]

As Lawrence Eppard and I make clear in *Inequality and Freedom*, freedom has a material basis in that it is an empty concept if it does not include the political and economic realms. For that reason, personal and political rights have to be matched by economic rights, and freedom must be defined not merely as an expression of self-interest but through the broader lens of social responsibility. This suggests connecting freedom and democracy with a revival of the social contract, on the one hand, and the further struggle to dismantle neoliberal capitalism on the other.

With the rise in hate speech, right-wing extremist violence, gerrymandering, the sabotaging of the voting process for Blacks, police violence, and staggering economic, health, and educational disparities, UN special rapporteur Fernand de Varennes stated that "the United States is becoming a darker, nastier, and more divided society."[38] It should come as no surprise that a number of organizations, from Freedom House to the European think tank International IDEA, report that democracy, at least what is left of it, is eroding in the United States.[39] The findings of the IDEA report challenge one of the most damaging assumptions about democracy held by many Americans. That is, they believe that democracy in the

United States is permanent, untouchable, incapable of attack, and not subject to being destroyed. Equally disturbing is the fact that both in the United States and around the globe, autocratic leaders no longer need to come to power by relying solely on force; they can also now do it through the ballot box.

This view of American exceptionalism is as dangerous as it is false. It breeds indifference and sets the stage for an overthrow of democracy in ways that will not be acknowledged or recognized by Americans. The second dangerous assumption about democracy is that democracy and capitalism are synonymous. Such a coupling constitutes an overlooked oxymoron; consequently, it is crucial for progressives and others to wage an educational and political campaign to make visible how the capitalist state produces ecological destruction, death-dealing forms of militarism, imposes massive degrees of poverty, reduces access to important social provisions and public goods such as childcare and meaningful work, and creates policies and institutions engaged in systemic racism and state terrorism.

CHAPTER SIXTEEN

Making Education Central to Politics and Everyday Life

In a different historical context, the Italian Marxist Antonio Gramsci stated that when a society is facing a crisis of authority it is often marked by a period in which "the old is dying and the new cannot be born; in this interregnum a great variety of morbid symptoms appear."[1] In this case, he was referring to Italy under the fascist rule of Mussolini. According to Gramsci, people no longer believed in the old order, but such disbelief did not guarantee a revolutionary change for the better. On the contrary, the interregnum or volatile period in which authority was in crisis also provided an opportunity for destructive systemic conditions to be born. The lesson here for the present is not despair or cynicism but how to take advantage of the breakdown of dominant authority and recognize what tools are needed to rethink the nature of politics and build a radical public imagination along with conditions necessary for mass struggle.

Old paradigms give way to new ones through the medium of culture, language, and education. It is in this space of communication and pedagogy that the incubation period takes place in which identifications are formed, consciousness settles on modes of recognition, and agency is constructed. Narratives emerge, stories change lives, and politics becomes a flashpoint. In this pedagogical space of uncertainty, radical ideas can be born, take hold, and shape a social order. We live at a time when the crisis of authority has given way to economic and political monstrosities, and one of them is neoliberal capitalism and its apprised embrace of fascist politics.

The lack of a radical mass consciousness makes all the more possible what James Meek calls "a future civil way in America taking the form of a smouldering, uncoordinated insurgency by pro-Trump conspiracists against a liberal reigning order of corporations, media, government, academia and metro society."[2] Meeks points less to an insurgency than to a counter-revolution buttressed by a culture of lies and lawlessness. Not only is a counter-narrative necessary but a mass social movement to implement it. Education is one of the fundamental spaces where the dominant narrative of an emerging fascist politics can be challenged, resistance organized, and the struggle over consciousness becomes a crucial pedagogical tool for social change. Let me be more specific.

Rather than wage war against neoliberal capitalism in the abstract, it is necessary to construct a political and educational campaign in which activists speak to people in a language they understand, one that makes visible the problems they face and provides them with a moment of recognition capable of altering their commonsense assumptions about how they deal with the problems they experience. This means addressing fundamental concrete problems such as the threat to social security, funding public education, abolishing student debt, providing free child care, implementing universal health care, providing a social wage for everyone, eliminating homelessness, dismantling the prison-industrial complex, curbing gun violence, making neighborhoods safe, massively reducing military budgets in order to expand programs to eliminate poverty, homelessness, food insecurity, and decaying infrastructures, among other issues. These deeply rooted issues begin not with abstractions about predatory capitalism but with a language in which people can identify themselves with the issues being addressed. Violence in this instance is visceral, felt, recognized, and familiar.

Education, both within and outside of schools, should offer a space where hard questions can be asked, people learn how to listen carefully to each other, and where educators and other cultural workers create public spaces where it becomes possible not only to "shift the way people think about the moment, but potentially to energize them to do something differently in that moment," to link one's critical imagination with the possibility of activism in the public sphere.[3] In this pedagogical approach, imagination moves beyond the realm of the aesthetic and abstract concepts and builds on it in order to reveal not only the visible workings of power but also how it hides in the shadows of silence and misinformation.

Furthermore, there is a vital need to wage a political and educational campaign to defend schools, a free press, and other institutions that provide the conditions for people to think critically, question authority, learn the tools for making informed judgments, and embrace what it means to be moral witnesses and engaged citizens. As a result, education would not be solely for training but for educating people to become critical and engaged citizens who can reflect critically about themselves, society, and the larger world; it also means learning how to question those in power, learning how to say no, and embracing visions that are courageous and imaginative.[4] It also means challenging those right-wing forces intent on destroying public and higher education, free speech, an oppositional press, and other rights and institutions.

Such a challenge would make visible how the eradication of local newspapers in the United States constitutes a death-blow to a democracy. As local newspapers disappear it becomes more difficult to hold accountable those politicians and corporations who engage in corruption. The defense of local newspapers is especially important given that the eradication of local newspapers has been linked to the corrupt practices of predatory hedge fund companies such as Alden Global Capital, which has bought out endless newspapers and then stripped them of their assets and sold them off.[5] There is more at work here than a savage form of asset stripping and gutting of newspapers; there is also the destruction of a free press by the titans of financial capitalism. Most importantly, there is the elimination of those informed resources, institutions, and public goods that resist the transformation of society into a shapeless landscape of capitalist rubble.

The urgent need to make education fundamental to politics demands a new language, a different regime of desires, new forms of identification, and a struggle to create new modes of thinking, subjectivity, and agency. It is important to stress repeatedly that direct action, cultural politics, and political education are essential tools to mobilize public attention as part of a broader campaign both to inform a wider public and create the conditions for mass struggle. Moreover, such campaigns must be international in scope, especially at a time when power is global, and politics are ineffectively local. Only a mass global movement will be capable of challenging the institutions and power relations that float above nation states, treating them mostly as resources to further the profits of the financial elite. Moreover, as Angela Davis has pointed out, it is imperative to have an international understanding of how fascism is spreading across the globe and how it connects countries as diverse as the United States and Brazil, on the one hand, and India, Hungary, and Turkey on the other. According to Davis,

> I would suggest that here in the U.S., if we are serious about being victorious over fascism, that we have to have an internationalist perspective. We can't simply focus on what is happening in Washington. We can't simply focus only on our domestic issues. We have to have a greater understanding of what is happening in Brazil, in the Philippines, in South Africa, in Palestine, throughout Europe.[6]

The threads that connect these various authoritarian regimes appeal to xenophobic nationalism, the call for racial cleansing, and powerful political pedagogical apparatuses that forge a discourse of hate, nativism, fear, and political violence as part of a broader effort to remake collective identity. In these circumstances, it is vital to acknowledge that education as an emancipatory force is central to politics because it provides the foundation for those willing to engage democracy as a site of struggle, which can only be waged through a consciousness of both its fragility and necessity. What educators and other cultural workers cannot do is look away, because the fascist danger that confronts democracy is not confined to the margins of society.

Yet far too many critics refuse to acknowledge how the ghost of a fascism that prevailed in the past is still with us in different forms and is becoming triumphant in the present. Education, cultural politics, and mass consciousness face an enemy in the current historical moment that is about to engulf us all. The necessity to take up the fight against a revamped fascism is no longer a matter of imagining a different and more emancipatory politics; it is an urgency that demands a revival of both an insurgent historical consciousness and the will to act collectively to usher in a future filled with socialist dreams of equality, freedom, and justice rather than the nightmare politics of an authoritarian present.

I am not suggesting that education alone will usher in an insurrectional democracy, but it will play a vital role in addressing the collapse of conscience, the call to unify isolated single-issue movements, and make clear the necessity for expanding cultural spheres and cultural apparatuses where the struggle over agency and politics takes place. What is clear in the current historical moment is that right-wing cultural politics have influenced and weakened civic culture with unprecedented success. That is, "the weaponization of culture and information has been much more successfully exploited by the neofascists than their disorientated opponents."[7]

A radical shift in consciousness on the part of the public is needed in order for matters of truth, justice, and science to offer the resources necessary to protect human life and sustain a critically informed public. Democracy cannot survive without a knowledgeable public and the institutions that provide skills, knowledge, and ideas necessary for extending the civic imagination. Learning how to think critically about our lives, others, and the wider world is both the basis of informed agency and one of the preconditions that enable individual and social change. Learned ignorance is never innocent. Facing a tsunami of lies, hope becomes senseless, and ignorance combines with rage and conspiracy theories as the first resort of the powerless. When shaping an authoritarian, populist mass movement, ignorance does more than expand the disintegration of political culture; it also makes possible the reproduction of the horrors of racial cleansing and violence as a tool of governance and instrument of political power.

Before the power relations and institutions of economic, religious, and cultural neoliberalism can be challenged, there is a need for mass awareness of the forces at work in destroying the ideological and institutional supports fundamental to a democracy. The late world-renowned sociologist Zygmunt Bauman insisted that the bleakness and dystopian politics of our times necessitate the ability to dream otherwise, to imagine a society "which thinks it is not just enough, which questions the sufficiency of any achieved level of justice and considers justice always to be a step or more ahead. Above all, it is a society which reacts angrily to any case of injustice and promptly sets about correcting it."[8] While hope has fallen on hard times under the dark shadow of the resurgence of white supremacy, a sense of collective passion and struggle is far from a historical relic.

In the age of galloping fascist insurrections, all of us have a responsibility, as Primo Levi, an Auschwitz survivor, once warned, to recognize that "Every age has its own fascism."[9] In a society where democracy is under siege, it is critical to remember that alternative futures are possible and that acting on these beliefs is a precondition for making radical change possible. At risk here is the courage to take on the challenge of what kind of world we want—what kind of future we want to build for our children. How might we reassert a notion of the social that reclaims through the radical imagination the terms through which we are connected to each other and the planet? What is the role of hope in an age of racialized visceral terror? Terry Eagleton furthers the importance of hope by arguing that "the only authentic image of the future is, in the end, the failure of the present."[10]

Democracy is in free fall and has reached a dangerous turning point. The horrors of a past committed to racial cleansing and a fascist politics are with us once again. But the tactics used in the past to fight fascism have to be rethought and updated. The challenge of changing public consciousness and the social imagination through the merging of political education and popular culture has to be aligned with the struggle to change material relations of power. There is more to consider here than the repudiation of manufactured ignorance, the scourge of white supremacy, and a corrupt political system. In the shadows of this escalating crisis, it is imperative to mobilize a multi-cultural, mass-based movement to uncover and fight on multiple levels this rebranded notion of fascism and its mounting wreckage before hope becomes an empty slogan and democracy a relic of the past.

CHAPTER SEVENTEEN

Insurrectional Democracy and the Politics of Education

America needs a massive movement for insurrectional democracy. The United States is in the midst of a cultural war infused by a counter-revolutionary movement that is waging a full-scale attack against ideas, truth, rationality, ethics, and justice. This is a site of contestation and struggles over minds, emotions, and modes of agency; it takes place in various institutions, cultural apparatuses, and public spaces that must be challenged, redefined, and appropriated as sites of resistance. As the social state collapses and capitalism constructs an unholy alliance with white supremacy, a fascist politics emerges that removes the language of maimed identities, pain, and rage from the structures of a savage neoliberalism while undermining the ideals and promises of a socialist democracy.

In part, this attack takes place through a cultural and educational politics that produces civic illiteracy, manufactured ignorance, moral decay, and historical amnesia, all the while promoting apocalyptic fears that feed off an exaggerated discourse of catastrophe allegedly facing white civilization. As I have mentioned previously, education in the broadest sense has become part of a cultural and political war zone and counter-revolutionary movement that now characterizes much of America. This is a counter-revolution built on lies, conspiracy theories, fear, and the drive for unbridled power. Its appeal to apocalyptic fears undermines shared values among different groups, produces a sense of anxiety and disorder, and reinforces the militarization of the police. It also contributes to the rise of the surveillance state, gated communities, the destruction of public goods such as schools, and intensifies the demonization of those deemed other, disposable, and a threat to white nationalism.[1]

A new anti-capitalist politics must arise against the regressive educational and cultural project at the core of this struggle. As the historian Heather Cox Richardson has argued, the struggle over education is tantamount to a struggle over the future itself. She rightly states that such a struggle demands "changing the way people think, and that we change the way people think by changing the way we talk about things."[2] It also necessitates making power visible and creating the pedagogical conditions that enable individuals to become critically engaged agents. Changing consciousness is a political and pedagogical task that connects learning to the tasks of changing how people view themselves as critical and active citizens.

In part, this means honoring a concept of hope driven by what the philosopher Ernst Bloch called the idea of the "Not Yet"— that space that refuses the absence of dreams, embracing instead the utopian presence propelling humanity into the future that has yet to be fulfilled.[3] For Bloch, hope "contains the spark that reaches out beyond the surrounding emptiness."[4] What is clear is that the "surrounding emptiness" produced under capitalism will not change merely through an alteration in policies. Any viable movement to build socialism cannot take place without a change in consciousness. This necessitates creating a formative culture whose aim is to produce social spaces and shared values that can fight back the tyranny of social atomization and fragmentation endemic to neoliberalism. It also necessitates rethinking the relationship between agency, knowledge, and collective resistance. Power must be understood beyond the structures of ideological and economic domination. That is, it must occupy a theoretical and political space of both educated hope and resistance, one in which ideas are articulated to power and action. Activist Nina Turner is on target in arguing that not only do progressive movements need to be unified, but they also have to acknowledge that ideas have to be connected to power, love, hope, and compassion. Quoting Martin Luther King, Jr., she writes:

> good ideas are not enough – we need to marry our ideas to power. We have to win. Reverend Martin Luther King Jr has

a great quote about this: 'Power without love is reckless and abusive, and love without power is sentimental and anemic. Power at its best is love implementing the demands of justice, and justice at its best is power correcting everything that stands against love.'[5]

There is no room for a dystopian, neoliberal pedagogy in a democratic society because it destroys the foundation for a formative culture necessary to provide the modes of shared sociality and social agents who possess the knowledge, skills, and values that support an ongoing collective struggle for democratization. In light of the current neoliberal assault on all democratic public spheres, along with the urgency of the problems faced by those marginalized by class, race, age, and sexual orientation, it is imperative to develop a politics that both challenges and rejects the dystopian "dreamworlds" of consumption, privatization, deregulation, and the relentless and brutalizing search for accumulating profits. At the heart of such a struggle is the need for new social movements, a fresh language for politics, and an intense struggle to reclaim the ongoing struggle for economic justice, equity, and freedom.

Critical pedagogy as a moral and political practice can provide the ideological pathways for creating alternative public spheres that sustain a democratic formative culture to challenge the neoliberal anti-utopian authoritarianism that generates massive social inequality, deepens market savagery, promotes massive privatization, and unleashes a global war against any viable notion of social citizenship and critical education. In its most democratic form, pedagogy is an act of enlightenment, protest, and intervention that is counter-hegemonic in its goal of teaching students not only to be critically informed, knowledgeable, and self-reflective about themselves and the wider society but also to know how to resist racism, colonialization, class inequality, and authoritarianism.

Articulating ideas and hope to active spheres of power and resistance represent a struggle in need of a new vision, one that merges the power of critique in multiple sites with "a positive, forward-looking program for real change."[6] Such a struggle must be both domestic and international. One possibility is developing a global mass movement in defense of public goods and a socialist democracy capable of challenging the free-floating institutions of finance capital, trade, and power relations. Global problems demand global solutions, and that means finding ways to create global political, economic, and educational forces that can bring the corporate, economic, and financial elite under political scrutiny, accountability, and ethical control before dismantling them altogether.

The central question here concerns what resistance might look like as part of an attempt to theorize the role of education in a democracy, the centrality of the merging of culture and knowledge, and the need to analyze education as a key site of politics. In what follows, I want to focus on higher education, because it is one of the few places still left to offer a protective space for critical pedagogy and learning, even though it has been under siege by right-wing conservatives since the end of the sixties. By safe space, I am not referring to a pedagogical practice defined exclusively through the discourse of therapy and trauma, but to a practice that creates a radical pedagogical space for students to learn how to confront a range of social and economic injustices. Safe spaces should be brave civic spaces where students learn to be "dedicated to the principle of thinking in order to act" individually and collectively within larger social movements.[7] They should function as pedagogical spheres for creating agents alert to memories of freedom, histories of struggle, and inspiring acts of collective transformation. Moreover, any talk of reforming higher education has relevance for how people learn and what they learn on a diverse number of other sites and political and social contexts. As a democratizing institution, the most important issue around its purpose should be defined by the question of what education should accomplish in a democracy.

Put differently, the purpose of the university should be on the side of democracy, not increasing the bottom line, which is what drives higher education today under the regime of neoliberalism.[8] Higher education needs to build a bridge between faculty, citizens, students, administrators, and the larger world. The broader public needs to understand the relevance of higher education (as well as public education) as an institution for the public good, rather than simply an adjunct of corporations, finance capital, and military interests.[9] In a time of incipient authoritarianism and an insurgency of white supremacy, it is especially important to raise the question of what public and higher education stand for or, as Paul Allen Miller argues, "where does the university stand [and] what does the university owe the truth?"[10] In the current moment marked by the proliferation of conspiracy theories, a culture of lying, and the assault on critical thought itself, Miller's question has enormous relevance for the entirety of institutions that shape American society.

What Miller is suggesting is that the university should take on the noble task of aligning itself with the search for truth, a task that must be matched by the infusion of learning with the spirit of civic culture, social justice, and economic equity. The university should not only be a place to refuse and resist the forces of neoliberalism by revealing its anti-democratic ethos and toxic austerity politics; it should also make an appeal to truth in refusing to compromise with oppressive forms of power, while at the same time exposing the financial and corporate interests at work in wider society. Educators, in this case, should function as academics and public intellectuals, as border crossers who can show how power is related to power and how knowledge can be used to address pressing social problems. They should exercise what Yale Law Dean Robert Post calls "democratic competence."[11] This suggests, for example, addressing the legacy and configuration of authoritarian and anti-democratic forces responsible for privatizing public services, eliminating public sector jobs, shipping jobs abroad, refusing to provide decent meaningful wages, curbing the power of trade unions, slashing retirement benefits, polluting rivers, poisoning drinking water with lead, and promoting tax cuts for the ultra-rich.

These issues are not limited to promoting the survival of higher education as a democratic sphere but also address concerns relevant for creating a more just, equitable, and meaningful life for everyone. Unfortunately, these goals have been under attack as the university has succumbed to the dictates of neoliberalism and, more recently, to aggressive right-wing attacks on tenure, unions, faculty and dissent, while at the same time removing control over curricula from faculty. This increasingly authoritarian war on tenure and the teaching of social justice issues is a full-fledged attempt by right-wing politicians to turn higher education institutions into factories of bigotry, conformity, and moral indifference.

As higher education has become more corporatized, the public perceives it less as a public good. Increasingly, the American people view it as a workstation for supplying labor for the global workforce. Several significant changes have taken place that undermine the democratic role of higher education. All of these must be reversed. First, higher education has been radically defunded because its potential role in providing free or cheap access to wider populations is seen as a threat to far-right foundations, conservative groups, and reactionary think tanks such as the Heritage Foundation, Manhattan Institute, and the American Enterprise Institute. These conservative think tanks engage in massive disinformation campaigns and "have made clear their attempts to undermine public education through vouchers, charter schools and opposition to teachers' unions."[12] As a vital public good, higher education poses a threat to these think tanks and conservatives who, since the sixties, have waged war against the democratization of higher education.

This war on higher education is also evident in massive increases in tuition and fees taking place in tandem with the public defunding of the university, contributing to the ballooning of student debt while making education less accessible to working-class students, especially Black and brown students.[13] In addition, faculty have been removed from having any control of the nature of their labor and have had their job security drastically reduced. In the United States, two-thirds of faculty are now on short-term contracts, living in fear and, in some cases, poverty. This attack on the power of faculty to control the conditions of their labor is part of a much broader assault on unions that went into high gear with the rise of neoliberalism, especially under the reign of Ronald Reagan, who as Governor of California campaigned against the United Farmworkers led by Cesar Chavez, and when elected president fired 13,000 air traffic controllers in the summer of 1981, effectively destroying the union PATCO.

What must also be noted by progressives is that the university's governing structure is not just top-heavy with administrators but is shaped by a form of managerialism modeled after a business culture. The university has become more than a model of corporate governance; it has become a high-powered factory run by a clueless managerial class more interested in grants, the bottom line, and profits than in high-quality education for everyone.[14] Neoliberal governing structures have turned destructive in their disregard for tenure, the rush for departmental mergers, and their ongoing disregard for academic freedom—a longstanding inheritance of the Reagan and Thatcher period when universities were increasingly defined through the lens of a business ideology and culture.[15]

Another attack on higher education takes place as corporate values replace academic values. Consequently, knowledge is reduced to a commodity, and any academic field or subject that does not mimic the worst form of profit-making and instrumental rationality is viewed as unnecessary or a liability. In this logic, there is no purpose in educating young people to be critical thinkers and engaged citizens, and connect what they learn to important public values and larger social issues. Nor is there an attempt to affirm education's critical function by connecting how knowledge is related to the power of both self-definition and social agency. Nor is there an attempt to encourage faculty to assume the mutually interdependent roles of critical educator and active citizen. This would mean providing the financial and intellectual resources necessary, along with the encouragement, to enable faculty to relate their academic work to alleviating human suffering, reduce the wastefulness of corporate barbarism, direct essential resources back to communities in need, and use their research to address the dangerous threat of climate change. None of these issues appear to warrant much consideration in the corporatized university. In fact, faculty who engage in this type of work tend increasingly to be punished—denied tenure, grants, and promotions, or simply terminated. In short, under the rule of neoliberal capitalism, the curricula are dumbed down, faculty are deskilled, overburdened, and stripped of their power, and students are reduced to the status of consumers and clients.

It is important to note that a similar war is being waged on public education. For instance, as reported in *Salon*, authoritarian leadership under the direction of right-wing educators and politicians affiliated with Hilldale College in Michigan are constructing a powerful conservative network of charter schools. According to Kathryn Joyce, charter schools:

> use public tax dollars to teach that systemic racism was effectively vanquished in the 1960s, that America was founded on 'Judeo-Christian' principles and that progressivism is fundamentally anti-American .... In an era of book bans, crusades against teaching about racism, and ever-widening proposals to punish teachers and librarians, Hillsdale is not just a central player, but a readymade solution for conservatives who seek to reclaim an educational system they believe was ceded decades ago to liberal interests.[16]

The success of the war against public schools serves as a petri dish for a potentially more aggressive war on higher education.

All these issues must be challenged by educators, parents, community members, and social movements outside the public schools and universities if education as a crucial force for a democracy is to survive. But such resistance must not only take place among students, faculty, and progressive administrators, it must also involve all those social movements who recognize that the same forces at work in destroying higher education are also undermining the viability of the welfare state, the environment, civil rights, struggles for economic equality, and any institution that furthers equality and social justice.

It is also important for the American public to acknowledge that education cannot be reduced to schooling in an image-based culture. Education must be universally understood as taking place in various locations and defined, in part, through its interrogation on the claims of democracy. As Ariel Dorfman argued, it is time to produce cultural institutions and empowering pedagogical conditions in multiple places, extending from the mainstream press to numerous alternative platforms, in order "to unleash the courage, energy, joy and, yes, compassion with which rebellious millions [can] defy fear and keep hope alive in these traumatic times."[17] Such sites are important in the efforts to engage education as a political force. Pierre Bourdieu rightly observed that "important forms of domination are not only economic but also intellectual and pedagogical and lie on the side of belief and persuasion [making it even more] important to recognize that intellectuals bear an enormous responsibility for challenging this form of domination."[18]

This is an especially important demand at a time when the educational and pedagogical force of the culture works through and across multiple places. Schooling is only one site of education, while screen culture, television, books, podcasts, magazines, the internet, social media platforms, and music venues are incredibly significant forces in shaping world views, modes of agency, and diverse forms of identification. The latter represents a new public sphere in which education becomes a powerful force for shaping consciousness, identity, and agency.

At a time when truth has become malleable, and people are being told that the only obligation of citizenship is to consume, language has become thinner and more individualistic, detached from history and more self-oriented, all the while undermining viable democratic social spheres as spaces where politics brings people together as collective agents willing to push at the frontiers of the political and moral imagination. Too many people across the globe have forgotten their civic lessons and in doing so cede the ground of history to the purveyors of lies, militarism, and white supremacy.[19] Terror comes in many forms, and one of its most powerful expressions is when people no longer have the words to either understand or challenge the world in which they live. Not only does such linguistic deprivation fail to ward off the plague of propaganda, but it also contributes "to an annihilation of the self and the destruction of the capacity to recognize the real world."[20]

If the university no longer engages in the search for truth, and matters of justice become irrelevant, "the university can become what it was under the Nazis, an institution that placed learning in service to a nationalist and militant culture, a mechanism for producing political legitimacy, ideological conformity, and economic value to be used and deployed by others."[21] Such a lesson extends far beyond the boundaries of the university. As educators and intellectuals, it is critical to remember that there is no genuine democracy without the presence of knowledgeable citizens willing to recognize and search for the truth, question authority, engage in forms of moral witnessing, break the continuity of commonsense, and challenge the emergence of anti-democratic institutions, policies, ideas, and social relations.

Making education fundamental to politics suggests that as academics, researchers, and artists, we ask uncomfortable questions about what Arundhati Roy called "our values and traditions, our vision for the future, our responsibilities as citizens, the legitimacy of our 'democratic institutions', the role of the state, the police, the army, the judiciary, and the intellectual community."[22] It is worth repeating that there is no democracy without the support and existence of parents, people, politicians, and institutions that define education as a public good and an indispensable public sphere. Educators, artists, intellectuals, and other cultural workers have a moral and political responsibility. That is, to put into place pedagogical sites and practices that enable critical agents and social movements that are willing to uphold the conviction that ecological destruction, mass poverty, militarism, systemic racism, staggering economic inequality, and a host of other social problems cannot be solved by leaving capitalism in place. Both higher education and other spheres of education must do justice to democracy and the conditions that make it possible by writing the future in the language of struggle, hope, equality, compassion, and the fundamental narratives of freedom and equality.

One of the challenges that educators, youth, artists, cultural workers, and others fighting for social change must address is how to make the political more pedagogical. This would necessitate connecting social problems, political and economic structures, and everyday experiences with the construction of an educated political consciousness marked by disciplined attention to meaning that enlarges "critical awareness of and of moral judgment in relation to [such experiences], an exercise of intelligence," which seems in short supply today.[23]

It is worth noting that this is not meant to suggest that critical consciousness is the endpoint of social change. Critical consciousness must connect theory and practice and in doing so establish informed analysis as a precondition for intervening in the world. The great Marxist theorist Antonio Gramsci provided a valuable lesson for educators in his insistence that it is essential to neither separate culture from systemic relations of power and state violence nor politics from the production of knowledge and identities shaped by such violence. This suggests that educators and other cultural workers begin to address how politics bears down on everyday life and becomes habitual through the force of its pedagogical practices, relations, and discourses. To be on the side of justice, educators must take seriously the notion that history is open and that it is necessary for people to think otherwise in order for them to act otherwise, especially if they take seriously that the role of higher education is to enable young people and others to be able to imagine and bring into being alternative democratic futures and horizons of possibility. This vision that is infused with a mix of justice, hope, and struggle has never been more important than it is today.

CHAPTER EIGHTEEN

Conclusion

In concluding, I want to return to the call for rethinking resistance in terms of the urgency of developing a combination of mass struggle and direct action. At the heart of this call is the necessity to merge a sense of moral outrage with a sense of civic courage and collective action. It is important to take on the challenge of initiating a period of mass awakening while articulating and connecting moments of political recognition, critical consciousness, and social awareness to the development of mass-based, collective struggles of resistance and transformation.

The United States has a rich and long history of protest movements. Going as far back as the sixties, people marched and protested against the Vietnam War, systemic racism, sexism, and the threat of nuclear war, among other types of oppression. These past movements responded with a combination of direct action and an array of cultural tools ranging from protest art to alternative media in order to speak to a broader public in an accessible, meaningful, and persuasive language.[1] In addition, a broader notion of cultural politics and education was crucial to all of these movements and is on display once again, though in updated forms amid a politics that is image-based and subject to the power of social media.

While history does not replicate itself in precise ways, the fruits of these past struggles, especially in the sixties, are manifesting themselves once again today. More recent protests have taken place against race-based police violence, ecological destruction, the assault on women's reproductive rights, the increasing number of reactionary policies initiated by a far-right Supreme Court, and the ongoing war being waged against LGBTQ rights gun violence, and public and higher education. All of these struggles have and continue to face massive resistance.

There is an urgent need today to reclaim and update the role of education in the broadest sense as part of the discourse of political struggle. This long unbroken historical struggle for racial and economic justice has continued, but for it to be successful it must be updated in order to address the crucial role that education now plays in reproducing and challenging intersecting forms of oppression while rejecting any notion of social change limited to existing forms of neoliberal capitalism. Such a movement cannot take place within the confines of the existing two-party system with its embrace of neoliberal capitalism.

It is also important to stress that if education in the broader sense does not become central to mass struggles now and in the future, there will be no radical change in society. In addition, what should unite a mass movement for radical democracy is not only a broad-based defense of public goods but tactics and strategies that involve direct action, political education, and cultural politics. There is an urgent need to mobilize workers, students, educators, and others across the country around popular issues related to democracy. One starting point is to point out that democracy and capitalism are incompatible and that the Democratic Party is not the answer to fighting the fascist politics now embraced by Trump, his followers, and the modern Republican Party. The left needs to organize around a formative narrative such as "radical democracy" in order to bring together different oppositional groups and be able to address in a clear message the enormous distrust and anger felt by many Americans. The left too often only speaks to itself. This challenge cannot take place under the leadership of the Democratic Party, which Sheldon Wolin once labeled as the "inauthentic opposition."

The Democratic Party is the party of Wall Street and can barely be relied on for even moderate social change. As the flag-bearer for neoliberalism and centrist politics, it has marginalized left demands within the party for policies that promote racial and economic equality, while "appealing to a public supposedly fearful of big-government policies."[2] This is evident in the fact that the Biden administration and the Democratic Party have done almost nothing to address a series of progressive proposals such as abolishing student loans, massively limiting the military budget, reigning in corporate/financial power, shoring up workplace rights, addressing massive inequality in wealth and power, forcing drug companies to lower prices, and providing Medicare for all, among other policies needed to improve peoples' lives while giving them more power in the future.[3] Nor is the Biden administration and Democratic leadership effectively protecting women's reproductive rights in light of the reversal of Roe vs. Wade. As Natasha Leonard points out in *The Intercept*. The Biden administration could at least "provide abortion services in states with bans."[4] As I write this, there is a global heat emergency taking place both in the United States and across the globe. Record breaking heat temperatures are producing massive fires. Biden's response to this climate emergence is shamelessly tepid and grossly inadequate.

The Democratic Party is wedded to protecting the institutional and cultural institutions modeled after Goldman Sachs and consequently have turned their backs on the myriad of economic and racist policies plaguing workers, the poor, and minorities of class and color.

At the very least, the Biden administration and the Democratic Party should raise the minimum wage to $15 an hour, kill the filibuster, go full force on climate action, protect the right to abortion, stop pushing a law-and-order discourse by expanding police funding, curb deportations of undocumented immigrants, prevent the right-wing from destroying public and higher education, protect voting rights, and expand the Supreme Court. Even if some action is taken on these issues, the Democratic Party's uncompromising support for neoliberal politics and economic policies will eventually serve to sabotage any meaningful reform.[5]

The failure of the Biden Administration and the Democratic Party, in general, is also evident in its inability to prevent a fascist politics from taking hold in the United States. Almost nothing is said about informing and arousing mass consciousness concerning the fascist threat posed by Trump, his political allies, and his followers. As the organization Refuse Fascism warns in its January 6 anniversary statement:

> The January 6 coup attempt demonstrated that fascism is not just the worst of a pendulum swing. It is an all-out assault on the rule of law aiming to strip democratic rights from whole groups of people they see as sub-human. Trump and his fascist movement have torn up the norms and thrown out the rule book, yet the outrage and hopes of people on the side of justice keep getting diverted into the very channels that are being eviscerated, and away from the kind

of deep, mass, society-wide struggle that is needed ... Biden and the Democratic Party have not stopped or slowed the advance of these fascists. Trump roams free to cement his hold over the GOP and run for president in 2024, while across the country, we are losing the right to abortion, voting, protest, history education, and free speech. Death threats against public officials have become routine, and Christian fascists on the Supreme Court [reversed] Roe v. Wade ... The Democratic Party has largely led people into inaction, passivity, and conciliation with fascism. This is a reality that must be confronted: Fascism can, and is, happening here and it cannot simply be voted away. The question remains, what will the decent people do? Will the future be fascist, or will we act?[6]

I want to make it clear that President Biden is not a malignant totalitarian in the manner of Donald Trump, and the Democratic Party is not a white supremacist party such as is the modern Republican Party. But Biden is a hawk in foreign policy and true to core neoliberal principles. As Paul Street has observed, Biden once "promised elite Manhattan donors in 2019 that 'nothing would fundamentally change' when he became president—a noxious thing to be caught saying in a nation where (even before the upwardly distributive Covid-19 recession) the top thousandth had as much wealth as the bottom 90 percent."[7] Without a doubt, Biden has a long pro-Wall Street record.[8] But the issue is not whether Biden is a politically hopeless centrist and neoliberal cheerleader as much as it is the failure of the Democratic Party historically and today to challenge the basic cruel and savage principles of gangster capitalism.

Under Trump, the modern Republican Party has defined itself against democracy and embraced fascism. On the other hand, the Democratic Party defines itself against Trump in the name of defending democracy and embraces a vision that amounts to supporting a "resurrected post-World War II political economy, complete with US global dominance based securely on a fast-growing US capitalism."[9] This is a politics at odds with its alleged support for democracy while disconnected from any viable notion of justice, economic equality, compassion, and the civic imagination.

The issue is not to improve the two-party system but to replace it with something better. There is an urgent need for a third political party in the United States that can organize and mobilize vast numbers of people by bringing together various progressive groups under the rubric of the banner of a future socialist democracy.

A broad working people's politics and party would not only add more stability to American politics but also bring to public consciousness the issue of socialism and the need to get beyond capitalism in order to develop a more democratic and egalitarian society.

What is at stake here are not just mass movements aimed at overthrowing the economic structures of finance capital but also forms of collective resistance whose aim is to combat the repressive formative cultures that enable state and corporate violence to be internalized and legitimized. There will be no successful movement for insurrectional change unless diverse progressive political formations come together and provide the pedagogical and cultural preconditions for creating modes of agency, identification, visions, values, and social relations necessary for ushering in a democratic socialist society. Hints of such collective resistance have been evident in a series of recent successful labor strikes and the merging of unionists and progressives who occupied the statehouse in Madison, Wisconsin, in 2011. Such resistance is also evident in the massive demonstrations taking place against the Supreme Court's reversal of women's reproductive rights. All of the latter provide a model for bringing diverse groups together in a show of direct action. Such actions offer a model for replicating such actions with regard to current battles over health mandates, banning of books, and the war being waged on LGBTQ youth.

At the very least, there is a need for more organizations such as the African American Policy Forum to monitor, provide resources, and work with movements involved to support academic freedom and expose and resist the war on public and higher education. There is also a need to connect the war on public schools, colleges, and universities with larger systemic concerns like inequality, mass poverty, persistent racism, and the attack on the welfare state. The Poor People's Campaign offers an updated effort to call attention to a range of injustices and violence related to economic and social inequality while calling for mass and direct acts of resistance. What is especially appealing in this movement is its call not only for fundamental economic and political rights but also its emphasis on what it states as a moral agenda—one that connects issues as far ranging as ecological devastation, poverty, and mass incarceration.[10]

Jason Pramas is right in stating that without a mass movement for fundamental change the "polity is well on its way to becoming a billionaire-ruled techno-feudalist state, as a growing number of political scientists from across the political spectrum are warning."[11] He is also right in asking: "Where's the mass sustained uprising we need to move this oligarchy back toward democracy? Nonviolent, to be sure. But militant. With clear and simple demands for improving the lives of millions of ordinary Americans."[12]

The good news is that a myriad of struggles are developing in the United States and other countries such as Brazil and Chile; they include calls for a living wage, food security, free education, jobs programs (especially for the young), the democratization of power, economic equality, and a massive shift in funds away from the machinery of war and big banks. Any collective struggle that matters has to develop an embryonic vision of the good life outside of the imperatives of unfettered "free-market" capitalism. More and more working people need to take direct action and get out in the streets, focusing on issues that bear down on their daily lives—issues that extend from free child and health care to calls for basics such as food, housing, a clean environment, and a politics that rejects control by the rich, religious extremists, and financial elite.[13] There are two strategic issues here that need to be taken up. One is the need to develop a wide range of accessible platforms to address people in a clear, inspiring, and accessible language. Marv Waterstone and Noam Chomsky are right to ask "where is the parallel competing messaging on the 'left' that draws upon the common-sensicial, material basis for political coalition, cohesion, and unity?" The left has to stop talking primarily to the choir. Secondly, acts of resistance need to be translated into more effective strategies. In part, this means using direct action to shut down institutions, even momentarily, to both educate people and produce new forms of resistance. One day strikes by teachers and students, medical personal, dock workers, and others would provide a powerful example of strategic resistance.

Too many progressives and people on the left are stuck in the discourse of foreclosure and cynicism and need to develop what Stuart Hall calls a "sense of politics being educative, of politics changing the way people see things."[14] There is a need for educators, young people, artists, and other cultural workers to develop a discourse of both criticism and hope in which people can address the historical, structural, and ideological conditions at the core of the imminent threat of fascist violence that has emerged in the United States and across the globe in countries such as Hungary and Turkey.

Nowhere will this struggle be more difficult than on the education front, a front in which a long-term organizing effort will have to take place to change consciousness, and once again, convince people that capitalism and democracy are not the same thing—and indeed are in conflict—offer up a new vision of democracy, and create the ideological and collective momentum to create a broad-based mass movement in which matters of class and race become foundational for addressing social justice issues and building movements. Single-issue social movements often speak to discrete problems and lack the willingness to embrace how the latter fit into a wider historical and relational understanding of power, politics, and interrelated systems of domination. We cannot address racism, sexism, the deterioration of public schooling, contaminated drinking water, homelessness, ecological devastation, and the collapse of the welfare state among other issues without addressing economic inequality and the concentration of wealth and power in the hands of a financial and corporate elite. Nor will isolated social movements be successful in enacting large-scale social change. What they may enact are reforms that may change some elements of the system but in the end do not challenge or change the totality of the political and economic structure of the existing social order.

Education and democracy fuel each other. If one falls, so does the other. A mass-based movement for public education via a national strike is urgently necessary and cannot happen fast enough. This fascist machinery of repressive education has to be shut down. As educators we cannot look away. We must recognize the severity of this threat because it is no longer slowly creeping up on us, it is already here. In the age of disimagination machines and media colonization, it becomes increasingly more difficult to think beyond the given, operate outside of dominant political landscapes, construct imagined futures, and produce collective visions that connect the radical imagination with militant acts of resistance.

The issue of who gets to define the future, share in the nation's wealth, shape the parameters of the social state, steward and protect the globe's resources, and create a formative culture for producing engaged and socially responsible citizens is not a rhetorical issue. This challenge offers new categories for defining how matters of representations, education, economic justice, and politics must be defined and fought over. Progressive taxes, educational equality, a social wage, and increased social provisions might add some weight to the responsibility of the welfare state, but it does not challenge the ideology and institutions of neoliberal capitalism. The end of capitalism demands a new language and vision that struggles for expansive democratic relations of power; greater worker representation and control over the conditions of labor and the workplace; the end of the capitalist cult of progress and expansion; free quality education and health care for all; the dismantling of the institutions of global finance; the complete elimination of class, racial, and cultural structures producing massive inequalities in wealth and power; among other calls for social change.

In a time of apocalyptic cynicism, the normalization of violence, and deepening collective despair, thinking about the future is more than a discourse of traditional aspirations. On the contrary, it is an interruptive and critical moment crucial to examining the horrors of a present descending all too quickly into fascism. Thinking about the future also necessitates the challenge of what it might mean to create a new language, vision, and motivation to embrace a future that imagines the fullness of justice, compassion, equality, and democracy. Thinking about the future is and should be an act of resistance.

The cry for justice, equality, and freedom takes on a new urgency and offers up new possibilities in the current historical moment. It infuses the present with the fire of wakefulness, longing for and hopefully producing a new language and politics for reclaiming our sense of agency, consciousness, and the courage to never look away. Hope expands the space of the possible and becomes a way of recognizing and naming the incomplete nature of the present. Reimagining the future suggests giving new meaning to the promise of a world without suffering, inequality, and the anti-democratic forces sprouting up like dangerous weeds. Thinking beyond the normalization of the present should offer the opportunity to rethink life, dignity, and human equality as they unfold to their fullest and always with others. Allowing the future to move beyond the shackles of the present should be rooted in dreams that reject the future as the present. It should be a time to talk back, beat down the fascist currents sweeping across the United States and elsewhere. Such a moment, filled with urgent possibilities, should be a time that brings together the fractured movements on the left in order to build a mass movement, new forms of direct action, and a political party that speaks with the people rather than against them.

In addition, it is crucial to acknowledge that protest and resistance are not enough. What is also needed are institutions with a vision of working for change outside of the existing framework of capitalism. As Stanley Aronowitz had argued for years, it is crucial for the left to develop alternative institutions that take care of people by addressing their essential needs, which range from healthcare and childcare to education, pensions, and other crucial supports. These might be called prefigurative zones of autonomy, whose purpose is to offer a model of what it means to change life. This suggests developing at the local level alternative communities that work to provide an alternative vision of what an anti-capitalist socialist society would look like.

I realize that these words of hope come at a challenging time in the United States, Canada, and across the globe. Civic courage, the social contract, and democracy itself are under siege. Struggling for a better world seems almost incomprehensible in a society where the pathology of power, privatization, and greed have turned the self inward to the point where any notion of social commitment and struggle for social justice appears either as a weakness or is treated with disdain. The role of governance has been removed from any sense of social responsibility. Freedom has partially collapsed into a moral nihilism that creates a straight line from politics to catastrophe to an apocalypse. Chaos, uncertainty, loneliness, and fear define the current historical moment. In too many cases, learned helplessness leads to learned hopelessness. A culture of consumerism, sensationalism, immediacy, and manufactured ignorance blinds us to how political and moral passions substitute sheer rage, anger, and emotion for a thoughtful defense of truth, the social contract, civic culture, a culture of questioning, and democracy itself. Manufactured ignorance is the precondition for consensual illiteracy, which kills the imagination by poisoning it with lies, consumer fantasies, the need for instant gratification, spectacularized instances of violence, data loops, and the death of historical memory. Manufactured ignorance has become performative, smothering the media with emotional minefields and affective blitzkriegs that dissolve the boundaries between truth and falsehoods, ethics and the unthinkable.

As I have mentioned earlier, there are counter instances of civic courage among young people, the Black and brown youth, teachers, health care workers, and others fighting social injustices and systemic racism while caring for the sick, dispossessed, and those bearing the weight of poverty, bigotry, and hatred. These inspiring and brave agents of democracy offer a history and sense of the present that allows us to greet the new year with a vision of what a different future would look like, one born out of moral witnessing, the social imagination, civic courage, and care for others. While it is true that we face the future at a time when social fractures and economic divides fuel a tsunami of fear, anger, falsehoods, conspiracy theories, and in some cases a politics wedded to violence, we need to summon the courage to reject normalizing such events. As such, we can never let hope turn into the pathology of cynicism or worse. Hopefully, the struggles against the existing state of tyranny will construct a visionary language as a condition for rethinking the possibilities that might come in the future, one that offers the promise of a sustainable socialist democracy.

Values such as freedom, solidarity, and equality need to "breathe" again, develop deeper roots, and renew an individual and collective sense of social responsibility and joint action. We need to throw out the crippling assumptions that turn freedom into a toxic notion of selfishness, hope into a crippling cynicism, and politics into a site of indifference, cruelty, and widely sanctioned forms of ruthlessness.[15] Facing the challenges of the present and the hopes that come with the future should give us a chance to reclaim the virtues of dignity, compassion, and justice. It should provide us with the opportunity to dream again, imagine the unimaginable, and think otherwise in order to act otherwise.

Professor Eddie S. Claude Jr., appearing on the Lawrence O' Donnell show on MSNBC in March 2022, reiterated the notion that America is more than an idea; it is an argument and battle over the very meaning and existence of democracy. He made it clear that America does not belong to the authoritarians who revel in white supremacy, the purging of dissent, the building of walls, and the death of democracy. Nor does it belong to those who, under the cover of democracy, wage a war against its most cherished and dangerous values. America is at war with itself, and that war cannot be won without a fight against the very real threat of authoritarianism.

As Jacques Derrida once put it, the fight is for the idea of a democracy to come, a democracy that may be in chains but still holds the promise of being unfinished. America as an identity cannot be handed over to those who believe that critically informed citizens, equality, and justice have no place in America. Nor can it be handed over to the apostles of neoliberal capitalism. At stake here are the democratic values, rights, and institutions that allow democracy to breathe. The fog of authoritarianism in its neoliberal white nationalist savagery and white Christian fundamentalism is getting thicker in America and across the globe. Fascist governments and networks now stretch from Russia, Brazil, and Hungary to Italy and Sweden. Our only hope lies in a vision and collective struggle that refuses to allow the idea and the promise of a socialist democracy to be still born.

Any struggle for resistance must create the pedagogical conditions that address the vital connection between agency and action. The great Frederick Douglass understood this when he stated in one of his most famous quotes that "knowledge makes a man unfit to be a slave." While it is generally accepted that power cannot be divorced from knowledge, it is often forgotten that agency is the central political category here and that at the heart of authoritarianism is the uniformed individual, an often isolated and depoliticized subject who has relinquished their agency to the cult of the strongman.

As the clouds of fascism once again appear on the horizon, it is more vital than ever to not allow history to repeat itself. My friend, the late Howard Zinn, got it right in his observation: "I can understand pessimism, but I don't believe in it. It's not simply a matter of faith, but of historical evidence. Not overwhelming evidence, just enough to give hope, because for hope we don't need certainty, only possibility."[16] This is all the more urgent given that the truth about America is being written in blood, whether we wish to acknowledge it or not. We have no choice but to acknowledge it and in doing so should summon up the courage to recognize, as James Baldwin once said, "Not everything that is faced can be changed; but nothing can be changed until it is faced."[17] The words of Baldwin and Zinn are more relevant today than ever before because they speak to a moment when democracy is fading and the problems we face are too urgent to look away.

NOTES

Chapter 1

1 See Chris Hedges, "The rise of American fascism," *CommonDreams* (June 27, 2022). Online: https://www.commondreams.org/views/2022/06/27/rise-american-fascism

2 Mike Levine, "'No blame?' ABC News finds 54 cases invoking 'Trump' in connection with violence, threats, alleged assaults," *ABC News* (May 30, 2020). Online: https://abcnews.go.com/Politics/blame-abc-news-finds-17-cases-invoking-trump/story?id=58912889

3 Judith Butler, "The criminalization of knowledge," *The Chronicle of Higher Education* [May 27, 2018]. Online: https://www.chronicle.com/article/The-Criminalization-of/243501

4 On white supremacy and systemic racism, see Kathleen Belew, *A Field Guide to White Supremacy* (Oakland: University of California Press, 2021); Also see David Theo Goldberg, *The Racial State* (New York: Wiley-Blackwell, 2001); David Theo Goldberg, *Are We All Postracial Yet?* (London: Polity, 2015). For a brilliant analysis of the relationship between freedom and whiteness, see Tyler Stovall, *White Freedom* (Princeton, NJ: Princeton University Press, 2021). For a superb theoretical analysis of race and difference, see *Stuart Hall: Selected Writings on Race and Difference*, ed. Paul Gilroy and Ruth Wilson Gilmore (Durham, NC: Duke University Press, 2021). For a brilliant series of theoretical interventions about race in a time of crisis, see George Yancy, *On Race: 34 Conversations in a Time of Crisis* (New York: Oxford University Press, 2017).

5 Alex Henderson, "Bipartisan interest group believes 'insurrectionist' Marjorie Taylor Greene is 'ineligible' for re-election," *Alternet* (March 25, 2022). Online: https://www.alternet.org/2022/03/bipartisan-group-marjorie-taylor-greene/

6 Luke Mogelson, "Among the insurrectionists," *The New Yorker* (January 15, 2021). Online: https://www.newyorker.com/magazine/2021/01/25/among-the-insurrectionists

NOTES

7   Cited in Tyler Stovall, "What is the relationship between democracy and authoritarianism?" *The Nation* (December 14, 2021). Retrieved from https://www.thenation.com/article/society/democracy-authoritarianism-david-bell/

8   Fabiola Cineas, "Donald Trump is the accelerant," *Vox* (January 9, 2021). Online: https://www.vox.com/21506029/trump-violence-tweets-racist-hate-speech

9   Jason Wilson, "US Militia group draws members from military and police, website leak shows," *The Guardian* (March 3, 2021). Online: https://www.theguardian.com/us-news/2021/mar/03/us-militia-membership-military-police-american-patriot-three-percenter-website-leak

10 Cited in David Remnick, "How Henry Louis Gates Jr., helped remake the literary canon," *The New Yorker* (February 19, 2022). Online: https://www.newyorker.com/culture/the-new-yorker-interview/how-henry-louis-gates-jr-helped-remake-the-literary-canon

11 There are too many sources available to document this issue, but some of the more interesting include Mary L. Trump, "Donald's Plot against America," *New Republic* (August 12, 2021). Online: https://newrepublic.com/article/163115/donald-trump-plot-against-america; John Dean, *Authoritarian Nightmare: Trump and His Followers* (New York: Melville, 2020); Anthony DiMaggio, *Rising Fascism in America: It Can Happen Here* (New York: Routledge, 2022); James Ridgeway, *Blood in the Face (revised new edition): White Nationalism from the Birth of a Nation to the Age of Trump* (Chicago: Haymarket, 2022); Bob Woodward and Robert Costa, Peril (New York: Simon & Schuster, 2021); Mary L. Trump, *The Reckoning: America's Trauma and Finding a Way to Heal* (New York: Faber & Faber, 2021). One of the best sources on the meaning of fascism is Daniel Guerin, *Fascism and Big Business*, second edition (New York: Pathfinder, 2000).

12 See, for example, the list provided by Thom Hartmann in "All the GOP has left is racism & that's a lie, too," *The Hartmann Report* (February 16, 2022). Online: https://hartmannreport.com/p/all-the-gop-has-left-is-racism-and?r=z0bje

13 Walter Rhein, "A disturbing percentage of Americans fantasize about racial cleansing," *An Injustice* (March 23, 2022). Online: https://aninjusticemag.com/a-disturbing-percentage-of-americans-fantasize-about-racial-cleansing-114c58a2824

14 Agencies, "At Arizona rally, Trump stirs racial tensions, repeats claim of stolen election," *The Times of Israel* (January 17, 2022).

Online: https://www.timesofisrael.com/at-arizona-rally-trump-stirs-racial-tensions-repeats-claim-of-stolen-election/

15 Pankaj Mishra, "Flailing states: Anglo-America loses its grip," *London Review of Books* (July 16, 2020). Online: https://www.lrb.co.uk/the-paper/v42/n14/pankaj-mishra/flailing-states

16 See, for instance, Philip Bump, "Tucker Carlson plays dumb on 'replacement theory' – then espouses it," *The Washington Post* (May 18, 2022). Online: https://www.washingtonpost.com/politics/2022/05/18/tucker-carlson-plays-dumb-replacement-theory-and-then-espouses-it/; Ryan Bort, "Quiz: Can you tell the difference between Tucker Carlson and an admitted white supremacist?," *Rolling Stone* (September 23, 2021). Online: https://www.rollingstone.com/politics/politics-news/tucker-carlson-great-replacement-white-supremacy-1231248/; Charles Blow, "Tucker Carlson and white replacement," *New York Times* (April 2021). Online: https://www.nytimes.com/2021/04/11/opinion/tucker-carlson-white-replacement.html

17 Phillip Martin, "Neo-Nazis target anti-racist doctors at Brigham and women's hospital, calling them 'anti-white'," *GBH News* (February 2, 2022). Online: https://www.wgbh.org/news/local-news/2022/02/02/neo-nazis-target-anti-racist-doctors-at-brigham-and-womens-hospital-calling-them-anti-white

18 Scott Remer, "Re-reading Theodor Adorno's *The Authoritarian Personality in an Age of Authoritarianism*," *Counterpunch* (March 27, 2022). Online: https://www.counterpunch.org/2022/03/27/re-reading-theodor-adornos-the-authoritarian-personality-in-an-age-of-authoritarianism/

19 Economist Intelligence Report, *Democracy Index 2021: less than half the world lives in a democracy* (February 10, 2022). Online: https://www.eiu.com/n/democracy-index-2021-less-than-half-the-world-lives-in-a-democracy/

20 Sara Repucci and Amy Slipowitz, *Freedom in the World 2022: The Global Expansion of Authoritarian Rule* (Washington, DC: Freedom House, 2022). Online: https://freedomhouse.org/report/freedom-world/2022/global-expansion-authoritarian-rule

21 Steve Phillips, "Ketanji Brown Jackson hearing reveals Republicans' racist fears," *The Guardian* (March 25, 2022). Online: https://www.theguardian.com/commentisfree/2022/mar/25/ketanji-brown-jackson-hearing-reveals-republicans-racist-fears

22 Dan Blaz, "Jackson endures questioning with racial overtones from GOP senators," *The Washington Post* (March 23, 2022).

Online: https://www.washingtonpost.com/politics/2022/03/23/
jackson-endures-questioning-with-racial-overtones-gop-senators/

23 Jack Ahern, "6 Republicans who used the Ketanji Brown Jackson
    hearings to throw out the wildest right-wing memes," *Salon* (March
    25, 2022). Online: https://www.salon.com/2022/03/25/6-used-the-
    ketanji-brown-jackson-hearings-to-throw-out-the-wildest-right-wing-
    memes/

Chapter 2

1   Brad Evans, *Ecce Humanitas: Beholding the Pain of Humanity*
    (New York: Columbia University Press, 2021), p. 3.

2   Ruth Ben-Ghiat touches on this issue, though she does not develop
    it enough, in Ruth Ben-Ghiat, "Jan. 6: A milestone of right-wing
    counterrevolution," *Lucid* (January 4, 2022). Online: https://lucid.
    substack.com/p/jan-6-a-milestone-of-right-wing-counterrevolutio

3   Kimberlé Williams Crenshaw, "The unmattering of black lives,"
    The New Republic (May 21, 2020). Online: https://newrepublic.com/
    article/157769/unmattering-black-lives

4   John Berger, *Hold Everything Dear: Dispatches on Survival and
    Resistance* (New York: Pantheon.2007), p. 89.

5   Amee Vanderpool, "We are still asking what role Hawley and Cruz
    played in Jan. 6," *SHERO* (March 25, 2022). Online: https://shero.
    substack.com/p/we-are-still-asking-what-role-hawley?s=r

6   Greg Sargent, "Opinion: Three big takeaways from Trump's missing
    Jan. 6 phone logs," *The Washington Post* (March 29, 2022). Online:
    https://www.washingtonpost.com/opinions/2022/03/29/trump-
    missing-phone-logs-key-takeaways/

7   Toni Morrison, "Racism and fascism," *The Journal of Negro
    Education* (Summer 1995). Online: https://www.leeannhunter.com/
    gender/wp-content/uploads/2012/11/Morrison-article.pdf

8   Ibid.

9   Crenshaw, "The unmattering of Black Lives."

10 David Smith, "The January 6 panel said Trump incited an
    'attempted coup'. Will it kill him or make him stronger?," *The
    Guardian* (June 11, 2022). Online: https://www.theguardian.com/
    us-news/2022/jun/11/jan-6-hearings-capitol-attack-trump-coup-
    analysis

11 Marshall Cohen, "Timeline of the coup: How Trump tried to weaponize the Justice Department to overturn the 2020 election," CNN Politics (November 5, 2021). Online: https://www.cnn.com/2021/11/05/politics/january-6-timeline-trump-coup/index.html; Ang Li and Rex Sakamoto, "Trump leaned on Justice Dept. to investigate election fraud claims," *New York Times* (June 23, 2022). Online: https://www.nytimes.com/video/us/politics/100000008414289/jan-6-hearing-trump-doj.html?playlistId=video/jan-6-committee-hearing-video

12 Achille Mbembe, *Necropolitics* (Durham, NC: Duke University Press, 2019). On disposability, also see Brad Evans and Henry A. Giroux, *Disposable Futures: The Seduction of Violence in the Age of Spectacle* (San Francisco: City Lights, 2015).

13 Laurence H. Tribe, "The risk of a coup in the next US election is greater now than it ever was under Trump," *The Guardian* (January 3, 2022). Online: https://www.theguardian.com/commentisfree/2022/jan/03/risk-us-coup-next-us-election-greater-than-under-trump

14 Jonathan Freedland, "The Republican party is embracing violence in the name of Trump," *The Guardian* (December 3, 2021). Online: https://www.theguardian.com/commentisfree/2021/dec/03/republican-party-democracy-political-violence-trumpism

15 Robert Pape, "American political violence: Why we cannot afford to ignore the American insurrectionist movement," *Chicago Project on Security & Threats* (August 6, 2021). Online: https://cpost.uchicago.edu/research/domestic_extremism/why_we_cannot_afford_to_ignore_the_american_insurrectionist_movement/

16 Thom Hartmann, "GOP now stands for trolls, vigilantes & death," *AlterNet* (November 23, 2021). Retrieved from https://ibw21.org/commentary/gop-now-stands-for-trolls-vigilantes-death/

17 Ibid.

18 Ruth Ben-Ghiat, "Demagogues don't debate: The GOP mimics Putin and Orbán," *Lucid* (January 18, 2022). Online: https://lucid.substack.com/p/demagogues-dont-debate-the-gop-mimics?utm_source=url

19 David D. Kirkpatrick, Maggie Astor and Catie Edmondson, "Trump praises Putin, leaving Republicans in a bind," *New York Times* (February 24, 2022). Online: https://www.nytimes.com/2022/02/24/world/europe/trump-putin-russia-ukraine.html

20 On this issue see the brilliant commentaries by Alexander Zevin "A normal war" *Sidecar* (March 31, 2022). Online: https://

newleftreview.org/sidecar/posts/a-normal-war?pc=1432 and Keith Gessen "Was it inevitable? A short history of Russia's war on Ukraine," *The Guardian* (March 11, 2022). Online: https://www. theguardian.com/world/2022/mar/11/was-it-inevitable-a-short-history-of-russias-war-on-ukraine

21　Amy Goodman, "Andrew Bacevich: Ukraine is paying the price for the U.S. 'recklessly' pushing NATO expansion," *Democracy Now* (March 11, 2020). Online: https://www.democracynow. org/2022/3/11/andrew_bacevich_iraq_connection_russian_invasion

22　Amy Goodman, "Tariq Ali on Ukraine, NATO expansion & how Putin's invasion galvanized a Russian peace movement," *Democracy Now* (March 9, 2022). Online: https://www.youtube.com/ watch?v=jAJ0VZDZoow

23　Rob Nixon, *Slow Violence and the Environmentalism of the Poor* (Cambridge, MA: Harvard University Press, 2011).

24　See, for instance, Angela Y. Davis, Gina Dent, Erica R. Meiners, and Beth E. Richie, *Abolition. Feminism. Now* (Chicago: Haymarket, 2022); Elizabeth Hinton, *America on Fire* (New York: W. W. Norton, 2021).

25　See, for instance, Matthew Desmond, *Evicted: Poverty and Profit in the American City* (New York: Crown, 2017); Elizabeth Hinton, *America on Fire: The Untold History of Police Violence and Black Rebellion Since the 1960s* (New York: Liveright, 2021); Virginia Eubanks, *Automating Inequality: How High-Tech Tools Profile, Police, and Punish the Poor* (New York: Picador, 2019).

26　See the classic text, Daniel Guerin, *Fascism and Big Business* (New York: Pathfinder, 1973).

27　On the billionaires supporting Republican politicians who seek to reverse US election results and support voter suppression legislation, see Stephanie Kirchgaessner, "Billionaires backed Republicans who sought to reverse US election results," *The Guardian* (January 15, 2021). Online: https://www.theguardian.com/us-news/2021/ jan/15/trump-republicans-election-defeat-club-for-growth; John Nichols, "Naming and shaming the organizations, corporations, and billionaires behind voter suppression," *The Nation* (July 23, 2021). Online: https://www.thenation.com/article/politics/voter-suppression-alec-billionaires/; See also Edward Helmore, "25 corporations marking Pride donated over $10m to anti-LGBTQ+ politicians," *US News* (June 14, 2021). Online: https://www.theguardian.com/ us-news/2021/jun/14/corporations-anti-lgbtq-politicians-donations-study

28 "Facts, inequality and health," Inequality.Org (March 14, 2022). Online: https://inequality.org/facts/inequality-and-health/

29 Press Release, "Ten richest men double their fortunes in pandemic while incomes of 99 percent of humanity fall," *Oxfam International* (January 17, 2022). Online: https://www.oxfam.org/en/press-releases/ten-richest-men-double-their-fortunes-pandemic-while-incomes-99-percent-humanity

30 Ibid.

31 Ibid.

32 Ibid.

33 Jesse Eisinger, Jeff Ernsthausen and Paul Kiel, "The secret IRS files: Trove of never-before-seen records reveal how the wealthiest avoid income tax," *ProPublica* (June 8, 2021). Online: https://www.propublica.org/article/the-secret-irs-files-trove-of-never-before-seen-records-reveal-how-the-wealthiest-avoid-income-tax

34 Michael Mechanic, "Another billionaire tax bites the dust," *Mother Jones* (March 31. 2022). Online: https://www.motherjones.com/politics/2022/03/biden-budget-proposal-billionaire-tax-dead-joe-manchin/

Chapter 3

1 A typically flawed example of this argument can be found in Dylan Matthews, "Is Trump a fascist? 8 experts weigh in," *Vox* (October 23, 2020). Online: https://www.vox.com/policy-and-politics/21521958/what-is-fascism-signs-donald-trump; see also Helmut Walser Smith, "No, America is not succumbing to fascism," *The Washington Post* (September 1, 2020). Online: https://www.washingtonpost.com/outlook/2020/09/01/no-america-is-not-succumbing-fascism/; For an excellent rebuttal to these claims, see Anthony DiMaggio, *Rising Fascism in America* (New York: Routledge, 2021) and Paul Street, *This Happened Here* (New York: Routledge, 2021); Henry A. Giroux, *American Nightmare: Facing the Challenge of Fascism* (San Francisco: City Lights, 2018). A number of prominent historians and politicians have labeled Trump as a fascist. These include Timothy Snyder, Geoff Eley, and Sarah Churchwell, the former US secretary of state Madeleine Albright and the Berkeley public policy professor Robert Reich.

2   For a weekly update on mass shootings in the United States, see the
    Gun Violence Archive at https://www.gunviolencearchive.org/reports/
    mass-shooting; also, see the weekly listings by Amee Vanderpool at
    SHERO: https://shero.substack.com/p/what-happened-was-310

3   Catie Edmondson, "The politics of menace," *New York Times*
    (November 22, 2021). Online: https://www.nytimes.com/2021/11/22/
    briefing/paul-gosar-censure-violence.html.For an excellent history of
    the rise of the radical right in the United States, see Nancy MacLean,
    Democracy in Chains (New York: Viking, 2017). For an analysis
    of the big money funding the "big lie" and the Republican push for
    authoritarianism, see Jane Mayer, "The big money behind the big
    lie," *The New Yorker* (August 2, 2021).

4   Oliver Knox, "Marjorie Taylor Greene says she's the GOP base, not
    the fringe. We'll see in 2022," *The Washington Post* (December 1,
    2021). Online: https://www.washingtonpost.com/politics/2021/12/01/
    marjorie-taylor-greene-says-shes-gop-base-not-fringe-well-see-2022/

5   Mark Follman, "In a pre-election video, Marjorie Taylor Greene
    endorsed political violence," *Mother Jones* (January 29, 2021).
    Online: https://www.motherjones.com/politics/2021/01/marjorie-
    taylor-greene-endorsed-political-violence-video-guns-elections-
    congress/

6   Ibid.

7   Brad Bull, "Michael Flynn says America needs 'one religion under
    God'," *Baptist News Global* (November 15, 2021). Online: https://
    baptistnews.com/article/michael-flynn-says-america-needs-one-
    religion-under-god/#.YaqEzdDMKmd

8   Carolyn Baker, *Confronting Christofascism: Healing the Evangelical
    Wound* (Berkeley, CA: Apocryphile Press, 2021); John Stoehr,
    "A growing threat is emerging from the theocratic wing of the
    GOP—but many liberals are missing it," *AlterNet* (November 16,
    2021). Online: https://www.alternet.org/2021/11/gop-theocracy/;
    Shirley R. Steinberg and Joe L. Kincheloe, *Christotainment: Selling
    Jesus through Popular Culture* (New York: Routledge, 2009). Chris
    Hedges, *American Fascists: The Christian Right and the War on
    America* (New York: Free Press, 2008).

9   Candace Rondeaux, "The digital general: How Trump ally Michael
    Flynn nurtured—and profited from—the QAnon conspiracy
    theory," *The Intercept* (June 27, 2021). Online: https://theintercept.
    com/2021/06/27/qanon-michael-flynn-digital-soldiers/

10 Hedges, *American Fascists*.

11   Annie Gowen, "A Jan. 6 pastor divides his Tennessee community with increasingly extremist views," *The Washington Post* (March 31, 2022). Online: https://www.washingtonpost.com/nation/2022/03/31/tennessee-pastor-extremist-politics/

12   Ibid.

13   Ibid.

14   Chris Hedges, "Mass politics must be rooted in class struggle," *The Real News* (January 25, 2022). Online: https://therealnews.com/chris-hedges-mass-politics-must-be-rooted-in-class-struggle

15   Geoff Eley, "What is fascism and where does it come from?" *History Workshop Journal*, 91:1 (Spring 2021). Online: https://doi.org/10.1093/hwj/dbab003

16   David Frum, "There's a word for what Trumpism is becoming," *The Atlantic* (July 13, 2021). Online: https://www.theatlantic.com/ideas/archive/2021/07/theres-word-what-trumpism-becoming/619418/

17   Ariel Shapiro, "The top 5 richest backers of Donald Trump," *Forbes* (October 30, 2020). Online: https://www.forbes.com/sites/arielshapiro/2020/10/30/the-top-5-richest-backers-of-donald-trump-adelson-hendricks-peterffy/?sh=61240d3f30ba

18   Cited in Thomas Homer-Dixon, "The American polity is cracked, and might collapse. Canada must prepare," *The Globe and Mail* (January 2, 2022). Online: https://www.theglobeandmail.com/opinion/article-the-american-polity-is-cracked-and-might-collapse-canada-must-prepare/?fbclid=IwAR0-A4OBQCbXr3FQYbkPsrKgR_mIhKChlaoam9ha78wiT7bvFuSkZD5f2Vw

19   See, for instance, Jane Mayer, "The making of the Fox News White House," *The New Yorker* (March 4, 2019). Online: https://www.newyorker.com/magazine/2019/03/11/the-making-of-the-fox-news-white-house

20   Dominic Boyer, "Digital fascism," *Society for Cultural Anthropology* (April 15, 2021). Online: https://culanth.org/fieldsights/digital-fascism

21   Thomas Klikauer and Meg Young, "The rise of digi-fascism," *Counterpunch* (April 11, 2022). Online: https://www.counterpunch.org/2022/04/11/the-rise-of-digi-fascism/

22   Ibid.

23   Jonathan Crary, "John Berger, enemy of neoliberal capitalism," *Politics / Letters*, [May 22, 2017]. Online: http://quarterly.politicsslashletters.org/john-berger-enemy-neoliberal-capitalism/

24 Jonathan Crary, 24/7 (London: Verso, 2013), p. 81. See also Kenneth Saltman, *Scripted Bodies: Corporate Power, Smart Technologies, and the Undoing of Public Education* (New York: Scripted Bodies, 2016).

25 Timothy Snyder, "The American abyss," *New York Times* (Jan 9, 2021). Online: https://www.nytimes.com/2021/01/09/magazine/trump-coup.html

26 Cited in Thom Hartmann, "Is Fox News 'The Greatest Cancer on American Democracy'?" *Thom Hartmann Medium* (December 15, 2021). Online: https://thomhartmann.medium.com/is-fox-news-the-greatest-cancer-on-american-democracy-ef876d388a0

27 Barton Gellman, "Trump's next coup has already begun," *The Atlantic* (December 6, 2021). Online: https://www.theatlantic.com/magazine/archive/2022/01/january-6-insurrection-trump-coup-2024-election/620843/

28 See Crary, 24/7

29 James Baldwin, *No Name in the Street* (New York: Vantage, 2007), p. 149.

30 Amy Goodman, "'The coming coup': Ari Berman on Republican efforts to steal future elections," *Democracy Now* (January 13, 2022). Online: https://www.democracynow.org/2022/1/13/gop_efforts_to_steal_future_elections

31 Ian Millhiser, "Where will abortion still be legal after *Roe* v. *Wade* is overruled?," *Vox* (April 12, 2022). Online: https://www.vox.com/23013308/supreme-court-roe-wade-abortion-legal-oklahoma-dobbs-jackson-womens-health

32 Timothy Snyder, "Op-ed: Words to fight the many faces of tyranny," *Los Angeles Times* (October 3, 2021). Online: https://www.latimes.com/opinion/story/2021-10-03/lessons-on-tyranny-timothy-snyder-op-ed

33 Jonathan Haidt, "why The Past 10 Years of American Life Have Been Uniquely Stupid," *The Atlantic* (May 2022). Online: https://www.theatlantic.com/magazine/archive/2022/05/social-media-democracy-trust-babel/629369/

34 The Editorial Board, "Every day is Jan. 6 now." *New York Times* (January 1, 2022). Online: https://www.nytimes.com/2022/01/01/opinion/january-6-attack-committee.html

Chapter 4

1 The historian Timothy Snyder has made this point many times in his
books, commentaries, and scholarly papers.

See, for instance, Timothy Snyder, "The American abyss," *The
New York Times* (Jan 9, 2021). Online: https://www.nytimes.
com/2021/01/09/magazine/trump-coup.html; Timothy Snyder,
"Op-ed: Words to fight the many faces of tyranny," *Los Angeles
Times* (October 3, 2021). Online: https://www.latimes.com/opinion/
story/2021-10-03/lessons-on-tyranny-timothy-snyder-op-ed;
Alex Henderson, "Journalist who predicted Trump's 2020 coup
explains why his supporters' 'openness to violence' is growing,"
Alternet (December 12, 2021). Retrieved from https://www.alternet.
org/2021/12/trump-coup-2655950826/

2 Philip Roth, *American Pastoral* (New York: Vintage, 1998), p. 137.

3 On the issue of inequality and freedom and the problematic notion of
freedom, see Lawrence Eppard and Henry A. Giroux, *On Inequality
and Freedom* (New York: Oxford University Press, 2022).

4 Richard Terdiman, "Deconstructing memory: On representing the
past and theorizing culture in France since the revolution," *Diacritics*
(Winter 1985), p. 16.

5 Gabrielle Bellot, "How black horror became America's most
powerful cinematic genre," *New York Times Style Magazine*
(November 10, 2021). Online: https://www.nytimes.com/2021/11/10/
t-magazine/black-horror-films-get-out.html

6 Sasha Abramsky, "Exploiting people's fears with surgical precision,"
The Nation (February 18, 2022). Online: https://www.thenation.com/
article/society/right-wing-crime/

7 Megan Zahneis, "'A naked attack': Texas Lieutenant Governor
pledges to end tenure for all new hires," *The Chronicle of Higher
Education* (February 18, 2022). Online: https://www.chronicle.com/
article/a-naked-attack-texas-lieutenant-governor-pledges-to-end-
tenure-for-all-new-hires?cid=gen_sign_in

8 See @Dan Patrick, https://twitter.com/danpatrick/status/
1493694009600053250.

9 Kathryn Joyce, "Fighting back against CRT panic: Educators
organize around the threat to academic freedom," *Salon* (March 7,
2022). Online: https://www.salon.com/2022/03/07/fighting-back-
against-crt-panic-educators-organize-around-the-to-academic-
freedom/

10 Ibid.

11 Jon Allsop, "The British public won't swallow the Tories' half-baked 'war on woke'," *The Guardian* (February 17, 2022). Online: https://www.theguardian.com/commentisfree/2022/feb/17/british-tories-war-on-woke-oliver-dowden

12 Ibram X. Kendi, "The danger more Republicans should be talking about," *The Atlantic* (April 16, 2022). Online: https://www.theatlantic.com/ideas/archive/2022/04/white-supremacy-grooming-in-republican-party/629585/

13 Martin Pengelly, "Outrage as Fox News commentator likens Anthony Fauci to Nazi doctor," *The Guardian* (November 30, 2021). Online: https://www.theguardian.com/us-news/2021/nov/30/anthony-fauci-josef-mengele-fox-news

14 Hannah Arendt, "Remembering W. H. Auden," *The New Yorker* (January 12, 1975). Online: https://www.newyorker.com/magazine/1975/01/20/remembering-wystan-h-auden-who-died-in-the-night-of-the-twenty-eighth-of-september-1973

15 Raoul Vaneigem, *The Revolution of Everyday life* (Oakland, CA: PM Press, 2012), p. 11.

16 Anthony DiMaggio, "The evidence of rising neo-fascism," *Refuse Fascism Podcast* (January 30, 2022). Online: https://refusefascism.org/2022/01/30/the-evidence-of-rising-neo-fascism/?link_id=0&can_id=f886cb99c76c72fa63ef56bf47bcb5db&source=email-anthony-dimaggrio-evidence-of-rising-neo-fascism&email_referrer=email_1428009&email_subject=anthony-dimaggio-evidence-of-rising-fascism

Chapter 5

1 Blake Hounshell and Leah Askarinam, "How many Americans support political violence?" *New York Times* (January 6, 2022). Online: https://www.nytimes.com/2022/01/05/us/politics/americans-political-violence-capitol-riot.html

2 Timothy Snyder, "How Hitler pioneered 'Fake news'," *New York Times* (October 16, 2019). Online: https://www.nytimes.com/2019/10/16/opinion/hitler-speech-1919.html. See also Jason Stanley, *How Propaganda Works* (Princeton, NJ: Princeton University Press, 2017).

3 Federico Finchelstein, *A Brief History of Fascist Lies* (Oakland: University of California Press, 2020).

4 Snyder, "How Hitler pioneered 'Fake news'." Online: https://www. nytimes.com/2019/10/16/opinion/hitler-speech-1919.html

5 German Lopez, "Donald Trump's long history of racism, from the 1970s to 2020," *Vox* (August 13, 2020). Online: https://www.vox. com/2016/7/25/12270880/donald-trump-racist-racism-history

6 Harold Myerson, "How racist are Republicans? Very." *The American Prospect* (October 22, 2020). Online: https://prospect.org/blogs/tap/ how-racist-are-republicans-very/; David A. Graham, Adrienne Green, Cullen Murphy, and Parker Richards, "An oral history of trump's bigotry," *The Atlantic* (June 2019). Online: https://www.theatlantic. com/magazine/archive/2019/06/trump-racism-comments/588067/

7 Report, "Deep divisions in Americans' views of nation's racial history – and how to address it," *Pew Research* Center (August 21, 2021). Online: https://www.pewresearch.org/politics/2021/08/12/ deep-divisions-in-americans-views-of-nations-racial-history-and-how- to-address-it/

8 Juan Williams, "Juan Williams: Biden is right—GOP is on wrong side of history," *The Hill* (January 31, 2022). Online: https://thehill.com/ opinion/civil-rights/592028-juan-williams-biden-is-right-gop-is-on- wrong-side-of-history

9 George Packer, "Are we doomed?" *The Atlantic* (December 6, 2021). Retrieved from https://www.theatlantic.com/magazine/ archive/2022/01/imagine-death-american-democracy-trump- insurrection/620841/; Thomas B. Edsall, "How to tell when your country is past the point of no return," *New York Times* (December 15, 2021). Online: https://www.nytimes.com/2021/12/15/opinion/ republicans-democracy-minority-rule.html; Ruth Ben-Ghiat, "Malcolm Nance: Welcome to the American insurgency," *Lucid* (January 5, 2022). Online: https://lucid.substack.com/p/malcolm- nance-welcome-to-the-american; Barton Gellman, "Trump's next coup has already begun," *The Atlantic* (December 6, 2021). Online: https://www.theatlantic.com/magazine/archive/2022/01/january- 6-insurrection-trump-coup-2024-election/620843/. The doomsday scenario has also been taken up by some conservatives such as David Brooks. See David Brooks, "America is falling apart at the seams," *New York Times* (January 13, 2022).

10 Sarah Steimer, "Insurrectionist movement in U.S. is larger and more dangerous than expected, research finds," *University of Chicago News* (August 12, 2021).

11 Hunter Walker, "Jan. 6 protest organizers say they participated in 'dozens' of planning meetings with members of Congress and White House staff," *Rolling Stone* (October 24, 2021). Online: https://www.rollingstone.com/politics/politics-news/exclusive-jan-6-organizers-met-congress-white-house-1245289/; See also Amee Vanderpool, "The seven hour gap in Trump call records, Part 1," SHERO (March 29, 2022). Online: https://shero.substack.com/p/the-seven-hour-gap-in-trump-call?token=eyJ1c2VyX2lkIjo3MDAzNDAsInBvc3RfaWQi OjUxMjM0MTA4LCJfIjoiM0lYaW8iLCJpYXQiOjE 2NDg1NjQyOTksImV4cCI6MTY0ODU2Nzg5OSwiaXNzIjoic HViLTk2ODQiLCJzdWIiOiJwb3N0LXJlYWN0aW9uIn0.l3 DpgnYJCLqEL940McOgRRE7bXdKAZLvnS3ezBa-aFU&s=r

12 Dan Balz, "Ginni Thomas texts reveal fears, motivation to overturn 2020 election," *The Washington Post* (March 26, 2022). Online: https://www.washingtonpost.com/politics/2022/03/26/ginn-thomas-texts-meadows/

13 Laurence H. Tribe, "The risk of a coup in the next US election is greater now than it ever was under Trump," *The Guardian* (January 3, 2022). Online: https://www.theguardian.com/commentisfree/2022/jan/03/risk-us-coup-next-us-election-greater-than-under-trump

14 Thom Hartmann, "Revealed: The racist plot to tear America apart," *The Hartmann Report* (November 30, 3021). Online: https://Hartmannnreport.com/p/revealed-the-racist-plot-to-tear see also, the classic commentary in David Theo Goldberg, *The Threat of Race: Reflections on Racial Neoliberalism* (New York: Wiley-Blackwell, 2011).

15 Annie Howard, "What good can dreaming do?" *Boston Review* (January 13, 2022). Online: https://bostonreview.net/articles/what-good-can-dreaming-do/

16 The classic text on the Reagan era is Rick Perlstein, *Reaganland: America's Right Turn 1976–1980* (New York: Simon & Schuster, 2020); for a useful summary of the forces at work in the unraveling of America, see Thom Hartmann, "How America is becoming unraveled," *Medium* (January 18, 2022). Online: https://thomhartmann.medium.com/how-america-is-becoming-unraveled-8b153e382d8e

17 Milton Friedman interviewed by Phil Donahue in 1979 on *The Phil Donahue Show*. Online: https://www.youtube.com/watch?v=RWsx1X8PV_A

18 See, for instance, Thomas Piketty, *Time for Socialism* (New Haven, CT: Yale University Press, 2022).

19 Pankaj Mishra, "Flailing states: Anglo-America loses its grip," *London Review of Books* (July 16, 2020). Online: https://www.lrb. co.uk/the-paper/v42/n14/pankaj-mishra/flailing-states

20 Henry Giroux, "The Powell Memo and the teaching machines of right-wing extremists," *History News Network* (October 1, 2009). Online: https://historynewsnetwork.org/article/117778; Michel Crozier, *Crisis of Democracy: Report on the Governability of Democracies to the Trilateral Commission Paperback—Oct. 1, 1975* (New York: NYU Press, 1975).

21 Jeffrey St. Clair, "Roaming charges: Is this tomorrow or just the end of time?" *CounterPunch* (January 21, 2022). Online: https://www. counterpunch.org/2022/01/21/roaming-charges-40/

22 Anthony DiMaggio, *Rising Fascism in America* (New York: Routledge, 2022) Paul Street, *This Happened Here* (New York: Routledge, 2022); I also take this issue up in detail in Henry A. Giroux, *The Terror of the Unforeseen* (Los Angeles: Los Angeles Review of Books, 2019). See also William Robinson, "How capitalism's structural and ideological crisis gives rise to neo-fascism," *The Real News* (February 5, 2020). Online: https:// therealnews.com/stories/capitalism-structural-ideological-crisis-neo-fascism; Michael Herer, "On Fascism and Capitalism," *Journal of Marxism and Capitalism* 11:1 (Summer 2020), pp. 48–58.

23 Mishra, "Flailing States: Anglo-America loses its grip."

24 Touré F. Reed, *Toward Freedom: The Case against Race Reductionism* (London: Verso, 2020), p. 103.

25 See: Zygmunt Bauman, *The Individualized Society* (London: Polity, 2001); Ulrich Beck and Elisabeth Beck-Gernsheim, *Individualization: Institutionalized Individualism and Its Social and Political Consequences* (London: SAGE, 2002); Henry A. Giroux, *Public Spaces, Private Lives: Beyond the Culture of Cynicism* (New York: Routledge, 2001).

26 Geoff Eley, "What is fascism and where does it come from?" *History Workshop Journal*, 91:1 (Spring 2021). Online: https://doi. org/10.1093/hwj/dbab003

27 Anne Nelson, *Shadow Network: Media, Money, and the Secret Hub of the Radical Right* (London: Bloomsbury, 2019). Essential to this issue is also Jane Mayer, *Dark Money: The Hidden History of the Billionaires behind the Rise of the Radical Right* (New York: Anchor, 2017) and Nancy MacLean, *Democracy in Chains: The Deep History of the Radical Right's Stealth Plan for America* (New York: Viking, 2017).

28 Ariane de Vogue, "Major 6-3 rulings foreshadow a sharper Supreme Court right turn," *CNN Politics* (July 1, 2021). Online: https://www.cnn.com/2021/07/01/politics/supreme-court-6-3-conservative-liberal/index.html

29 Jane Mayer, "The slime machine targeting dozens of Biden nominees," *The New Yorker* (April 16, 2022). Online: https://www.newyorker.com/news/a-reporter-at-large/the-slime-machine-targeting-dozens-of-biden-nominees

Chapter 6

1   Ashley Parker and Josh Dawsey, "Trump's cable cabinet: New texts reveal the influence of Fox hosts on previous White House." *The Washington Post* (January 9, 2022). Online: https://www.washingtonpost.com/politics/trump-cable-cabinet/2022/01/09/96fac488-6fe6-11ec-b9fc-b394d592a7a6_story.html

2   Martin Pengelly, "Rudy Giuliani and Michael Flynn to see honorary university degrees revoked," *The Guardian* (January 22, 2022). Online: https://www.theguardian.com/us-news/2022/jan/22/rudy-giuliani-michael-flynn-honorary-university-degrees-revoked; Dan Mangan, "Steve Bannon's podcast barred from Twitter after he made beheading comment about Fauci, FBI Director Wray," CNBC (November 5, 2020). Online: https://www.cnbc.com/2020/11/05/steve-bannon-makes-beheading-comment-about-fauci-on-war-room-podcast-.html

3   Andrew Kaczynski and Chris Massie, "White nationalists see advocate in Steve Bannon who will hold Trump to his campaign promises," *CNN Politics* (November 15, 2016). Online: https://www.cnn.com/2016/11/14/politics/white-nationalists-on-bannon/

4   John Gills cited in Jorge Mariscal, "Lethal and compassionate: The militarization of culture," *CounterPunch* (May 3, 2003), online www.counterpunch.org/mariscal0502003.html

5   James Risen, "Jan. 6 hearings seek to remind a forgetful nation about the day Donald Trump almost engineered a coup," *The Intercept* (June 10, 2022). Online: https://theintercept.com/2022/06/10/january-6-committee-hearings-trump-insurrection/

6   Chauncey DeVega, "The Jan. 6 anniversary: How the media failed—and still can't admit it," *Salon* (January 14, 2022). Online: https://www.salon.com/2022/01/14/the-jan-6-anniversary-how-the-media-failed--and-still-cant-admit-it/

7   Pankaj Mishra, "Responses to the invasion of Ukraine," *London Review of Books* (44:6 ((March 24, 2022), p. 14.

8   William D. Hartung and Julia Gledhill, "The new gold rush: How Pentagon contractors are cashing in on the Ukraine crisis," *TomDispatch* (April 17, 2022). Online: https://tomdispatch. com/the-new-gold-rush/?utm_source=TomDispatch&utm_ campaign=67bc85aa1c-EMAIL_CAMPAIGN_2021_07_13_02_04_ COPY_01&utm_medium=email&utm_term=0_1e41682ade-67bc85aa1c-308840025

9   Jackson Lears, "Responses to the invasion of Ukraine," *London Review of Books* (44:6 ((March 24, 2022), p. 13.

10   Jackson Lears, "The forgotten crime of war itself," *New York Review of Books* (April 21, 2022). Online: https://www.nybooks.com/ articles/2022/04/21/the-forgotten-crime-of-war-itself-samuel-moyn-lears/

11   Thom Hartmann, "Best of TomDispatch, Engelhardt, Washington's wedding album from hell," *TomDispatch* (April 10, 2022). Online: https://tomdispatch.com/bride-and-boom/?utm_source=TomDispatch&utm_campaign=a91ae2af36-EMAIL_CAMPAIGN_2021_07_13_02_04_COPY_01&utm_ medium=email&utm_term=0_1e41682ade-a91ae2af36-308840025

12   Mary Kaldor, "How to free hostages: War, negotiation, or law-enforcement," *Open Democracy* (September 28, 2007). Online: https://www.opendemocracy.net/en/article_2127jsp/

13   Rashawn Ray, "The Russian invasion of Ukraine shows racism has no boundaries," *Brookings* (March 3, 2022). Online: https://www. brookings.edu/blog/how-we-rise/2022/03/03/the-russian-invasion-of-ukraine-shows-racism-has-no-boundaries/

14   Rafia Zakaria, "Ukraine war exposes European racism," *The Statesman* (April 9, 2022). Online: https://www.thestatesman.com/ opinion/ukraine-war-exposes-european-racism-1503054718.html

15   Harper Lambert, "CBS reporter calls Ukraine 'relatively civilized' as opposed to Iraq and Afghanistan, outrage ensues (Video)," *The Wrap* (February 26, 2022). Online: https://www.thewrap.com/cbs-charlie-dagata-backlash-ukraine-civilized/

16   Moustafa Bayoumi, "They are 'civilised' and 'look like us': The racist coverage of Ukraine," *The Guardian* (March 2, 2022). Online: https://www.theguardian.com/commentisfree/2022/mar/02/civilised-european-look-like-us-racist-coverage-ukraine

17   Ibid.

18 Martin Luther King, Jr., Address in acceptance of Nobel Peace Prize (December 10, 1964). Online: https://www.nobelprize.org/prizes/ peace/1964/king/acceptance-speech/

19 Rev. Dr. Martin Luther King, Jr., "Remaining awake through a great revolution," *Martin Luther King, Jr. at Oberlin* (June 1965). Online: https://www2.oberlin.edu/external/EOG/BlackHistoryMonth/MLK/ CommAddress.html

Chapter 7

1 Henry A. Giroux, *American Nightmare: Facing the Challenge of Fascism* (San Francisco: City Lights, 2017).

Paul Street, "26 flavors of anti-antifascism, Part 1," *Counterpunch* (February 7, 2021). Online: https://www.counterpunch. org/2021/02/07/the-anatomy-of-fascism-denial/; Anthony DiMaggio, *Rising Fascism in America: It Can Happen Here* (New York: Routledge, 2022).

2 On persistent racism in America, see Eddie S. Claude, Jr. *Democracy in Black: How Race Still Enslaves the American Soul* (New York: Crown, 2016). On racist police violence and Black rebellion, see Elizabeth Hinton, *America on Fire* (New York: Liveright Publishing, 2021).

3 C. Wright Mills, "The Cultural Apparatus," in *The Politics of Truth: Selected Writings of C. Wright Mills*, ed. John H. Summers (Oxford: Oxford University Press, 2008), p. 204.

4 Achille Mbembe, "Necropolitics," trans. Libby Meintjes, *Public Culture*, 15:1 (2003), pp. 39–40.

5 See, for instance, Matthew Desmond, *Evicted: Poverty and Profit in the American City* (New York: Crown, 2017); Elizabeth Hinton, *America on Fire: The Untold History of Police Violence and Black Rebellion since the 1960s* (New York: Liveright, 2021); Virginia Eubanks, *Automating Inequality: How High-Tech Tools Profile, Police, and Punish the Poor* (New York: Picador, 2019).

6 Russ Choma, "Fox News invites Trump on to whitewash the January 6 insurrection," *Mother Jones* (July 11, 2021). Online: https://www. motherjones.com/politics/2021/07/fox-news-trump-bartiromo- whitewashing-january-6-insurrection/

7 Holmes Lybrand, "Fact checking claims January 6 was not an armed insurrection," *CNN Politics* (July 28, 2021). Online: https://www. cnn.com/2021/07/28/politics/armed-insurrection-january-6-guns-

fact-check/index.html; see also, Jonathan Chait, "Trump defends insurrectionists trying to hang Mike Pence as 'common sense'" *New York Magazine*, [November 12, 2021]. Retrieved from https://nymag. com/intelligencer/2021/11/trump-defends-hang-mike-pence-common-sense-january-6-insurrection-riot.html

8   Jenni Fink, "Trump says, 'real insurrection' happened on election day, praises Pence's Jan. 6 comments," *Newsweek* (October 6, 2021). Retrieved from https://www.newsweek.com/trump-says-real-insurrection-happened-election-day-praises-pences-jan-6-comments–1636196

9   Josh Dawsey, "Trump deflects blame for Jan. 6 silence, says he wanted to march to Capitol," *The Washington Post* (April 7, 2022). Online: https://www.washingtonpost.com/politics/2022/04/07/trump-interview-jan6/

10   Jonathan Edwards, "Georgia Republicans planned a vigil for 'J6 Patriots' on Jan. 6. One critic called it an 'homage to treason'," *The Washington Post* (January 6, 2022). Online: https://www. washingtonpost.com/nation/2022/01/06/georgia-republicans-capitol-riot-anniversary/

11   Ibid.

12   Editorial, "The insurrection, one year on," *The Economist* (January 8, 2021). Online: from https://www.economist.com/united-states/the-insurrection-one-year-on/21807018

13   Ibid.

14   Thom Hartmann, "GOP now stands for trolls, vigilantes & death," *AlterNet* (November 23, 2021). Online: https://ibw21.org/ commentary/gop-now-stands-for-trolls-vigilantes-death/

15   Noam Chomsky, "Noam Chomsky: GOP's soft coup is still underway one year after Capitol assault," *Truthout* (January 6, 2022). Online: https://truthout.org/articles/noam-chomsky-gops-soft-coup-is-still-underway-one-year-after-capitol-assault/

16   Ibid.

17   Fintan O'Toole, "The Trump inheritance," *The New York Review* (February 25, 2021). Online https://www.nybooks.com/ articles/2021/02/25/trump-inheritance/

18   Rick Halsen, "My new draft paper: 'Identifying and minimizing the risk of election subversion and stolen elections in the contemporary United States'," Election Law Blog (September 22, 2021). Online: https://electionlawblog.org/?p=124686

19 Spencer Bokat-Lindell, "Will 2024 be the year American democracy dies?" *New York Times* (September 30, 2021). Online: https://www.nytimes.com/2021/09/30/opinion/american-democracy-2024.html

20 Heather Cox Richardson, "January 17, 2022," *Letters from an American* (January 18, 2022). Online: https://heathercoxrichardson.substack.com/p/january-17-2022

21 George Packer, "Are we doomed?" *The Atlantic* (December 6, 2021). Retrieved from https://www.theatlantic.com/magazine/archive/2022/01/imagine-death-american-democracy-trump-insurrection/620841/

22 Some of the more prominent theorists of a coming civil war in the United States include Barbara F. Walter, *How Civil Wars Start: And How to Stop Them* (New York: Crown, 2022); Steven Marche, *The Next Civil War: Dispatches from the American Future* (New York: Simon & Schuster, 2022); David Theo Goldberg, *Dread* (London: Polity, 2021). See also the commentary by Malcolm Nance in Ruth Ben-Ghiat, "Malcolm Nance: Welcome to the American Insurgency," *Lucid* (January 5, 2022). Online: https://lucid.substack.com/p/malcolm-nance-welcome-to-the-american

23 Ibid. Packer, "Are we doomed?"

24 A number of factors make the possibility of a civil war possible; see William G. Gale and Darrell M. West, "Is the US headed for another Civil War?" Brookings Institute (September 16, 2021). Online: https://www.brookings.edu/blog/fixgov/2021/09/16/is-the-us-headed-for-another-civil-war/

Chapter 8

1 Lincoln Mitchell, "The Jan. 6 Capitol attack brought up lots of absurd casual talk of a new civil war brewing," *Think* (January 6, 2022). Online: https://www.nbcnews.com/think/opinion/jan-6-capitol-attack-brought-lots-absurd-casual-talk-new-ncna1286940

2 Michael Gerson, "The threat of violence now infuses GOP politics. We should all be afraid," *The Washington Post* (May 20, 2021). Online: https://www.washingtonpost.com/opinions/2021/05/20/trump-republicans-violent-threats-election-2024/. See also Ruth Ben-Ghiat, "The GOP wants to destroy politics as we know it. Violence and lies will fill the vacuum," *Lucid* (November 23, 2021). Online: https://lucid.substack.com/p/the-gop-wants-to-destroy-politics

3   Zak Cheney-Rice, "Can Republicans commit voter fraud?"
    New York Magazine (March 12, 2022). Online: https://nymag.com/
    intelligencer/2022/03/voter-fraud-mark-meadows.html

4   Patrick Cockburn, "The Republican Party has turned fascist and is
    now the most dangerous threat in the world," *Independent* (June 18,
    2021). Online: https://www.independent.co.uk/voices/republican-
    party-donald-trump-voter-suppression-b1868426.html

5   Fintan O'Toole, "Beware prophecies of civil war," *The Atlantic*
    (December 16, 2021). Retrieved from https://www.theatlantic.com/
    magazine/archive/2022/01/america-civil-war-prophecies/620850

6   Fintan O'Toole, "Beware prophecies of civil war," *The Atlantic*
    (December 16, 2021). Retrieved from https://www.theatlantic.com/
    magazine/archive/2022/01/america-civil-war-prophecies/620850

7   This inversion can be attributed to Michel Foucault *in Society Must
    be Defended: Lectures at the College de France*, trans. D. Macey
    (London: Penguin Books, 2004).

8   N. Velásquez, R. Leahy, N. Johnson Restrepo, Y. Lupu, R. Sear,
    N. Gabriel, O. K. Jha, B. Goldberg, and N. F. Johnson, "Online
    hate network spreads malicious COVID-19 content outside the
    control of individual social media platforms," *Scientific Reports*
    (June 15, 2021). Online: https://www.nature.com/articles/s41598-
    021-89467–y; Sergio Andres Castano-Pulgarín, Natalia Suarez-
    Betancur, Luz Magnolia Tilano Vega, and Harvey Mauricio Herrera
    Lopez, "Internet, social media and online hate speech. Systematic
    review," *Science Direct*, vol. 58. (April 6, 2021). Online: https://doi.
    org/10.1016/j.avb.2021.101608

9   Jonathan Crary, "John Berger, enemy of neoliberal capitalism,"
    Politics / Letters (May 22, 2017). Online: http://quarterly.
    politicsslashletters.org/john-berger-enemy-neoliberal-capitalism/

10 Ibid.

11 Ibid.

12 David Theo Goldberg, *Dread: Facing a Futureless Future* (London:
    Polity, 2021), p. 179. On the stats, see Aaron Blake, "39 percent
    of election deniers say violence might be needed to save America,"
    The Washington Post (November 1, 2021). Online: https://www.
    washingtonpost.com/politics/2021/11/01/4-10-who-say-election-was-
    stolen-trump-say-violence-might-be-needed-save-america/

13 Ibid., pp. 179, 183.

14 YouTube, "Former President Donald Trump speaks at 'Save America'
    rally in Conroe, Texas," *YouTube.com* (January 31, 2022). Online:
    https://www.youtube.com/watch?v=LvlcJDCYJh0

15 Martin Pengelly, "Trump pardon promise for Capitol rioters 'stuff of dictators' – Nixon aide," *The Guardian* (January 30, 2022). Online: https://www.theguardian.com/us-news/2022/jan/30/trump-pardon-promise-capitol-rioters-dictators-john-dean-nixon

16 Karen Tumulty, "A party that censures its defenders of the Constitution has lost its way," *The Washington Post* (February 5, 2022). Online: https://www.washingtonpost.com/opinions/2022/02/05/what-the-cheney-censure-tells-us-about-republican-party/

17 Michael S. Schmidt and Luke Broadwater, "Officers' injuries, including concussions, show scope of violence at Capitol riot," *New York Times* (July 11, 2021). Online: https://www.nytimes.com/2021/02/11/us/politics/capitol-riot-police-officer-injuries.html

18 Jeremy Best, "Framing political violence as patriotic is even more dangerous than it sounds," *The Washington Post* (November 10, 2021). Online: https://www.washingtonpost.com/outlook/2021/11/10/framing-political-violence-patriotic-is-even-more-dangerous-than-it-sound/

19 Heather Cox, "Letters from an American," *Substack* (February 14, 2022). Online: https://heathercoxrichardson.substack.com/p/february-14-2022?r=f0dw

20 Ibid.

21 Anthony DiMaggio, "Vigilantes on parade: Right-wing extremism and the threat of national implosion," *CounterPunch* (November 24, 2021). Online: https://www.counterpunch.org/2021/11/24/vigilantes-on-parade-right-wing-extremism-and-the-threat-of-national-implosion/

22 Fabiola Cineas, "Donald Trump is the accelerant," *Vox* (January 9, 2021). Online: https://www.vox.com/21506029/trump-violence-tweets-racist-hate-speech; Rebecca Traister, "The betrayal of Roe," *New York Magazine: Intelligencer* (December 2021). Online: https://nymag.com/intelligencer/2021/12/the-betrayal-of-roe.html

23 Staff and Agencies, "Republican Thomas Massie condemned for Christmas guns photo," *The Guardian* (December 5, 2021). Online: https://www.theguardian.com/us-news/2021/dec/05/republican-thomas-massie-condemned-for-christmas-guns-photo-congressman-michigan-school-shooting

24 Lisa Lerer and Astead W. Herndon, "Menace, as a political tool, enters the Republican mainstream," *The New York Times* (November 12, 2021). Retrieved from https://www.nytimes.com/2021/11/12/us/politics/republican-violent-rhetoric.html

25 Will Bunch, "At Texas rally, Trump all but promised a racially charged civil war if he's indicted," *The Philadelphia* (January 30, 2022). Online: https://www.inquirer.com/opinion/commentary/donald-trump-rally-conroe-texas-pardons-20220130.html

26 Ibid.

27 YouTube, "Former President Donald Trump speaks at 'Save America' rally in Conroe, Texas," *YouTube.com* (January 31, 2022). Online: https://www.youtube.com/watch?v=LvlcJDCYJh0

28 Bunch, "Texas Rally."

29 Fabiola Cineas, "Buffalo, seven weeks after the massacre," VOX (July 5, 2022). Online: https://www.vox.com/23189892/buffalo-mass-shooting-tops-supermarket

30 Paul Street, "On mass political inattention," *Counterpunch* (October 29, 2021). Online: https://www.counterpunch.org/2021/10/29/on-mass-political-inattention/?fbclid=IwAR0VDQAJOaBp0nMdtiwl0Y1JVcYcnGuBweKA3hvTK113A-WmUExGsMpixTA

Chapter 9

1 Ralph Nader, "Know this, Trump's attempted coup on Jan. 6 was just practice,' *Common Dreams* (December 14, 2021). Online: https://www.commondreams.org/views/2021/12/14/know-trumps-attempted-coup-jan-6-was-just-practice

2 Jean Seaton, "Why Orwell's 1984 could be about now," *BBC.com* (May 7, 2018) Online: https://www.bbc.com/culture/article/20180507-why-orwells-1984-could-be-about-now

3 Chauncey DeVega, "Irish author Fintan O'Toole explains the 'suspension of disbelief' that made Trump's destruction of America possible," *Alternet* (May 26, 2020) Online https://www.alternet.org/2020/05/irish-author-fintan-otoole-explains-the-suspension-of-disbelief-that-made-trumps-destruction-of-america-possible/

4 Jonathan Crary, *Scorched Earth: Beyond the Digital Age to a Post-Capitalist World* (London: Verso, 2022).

5 Thomas Klikauer and Meg Young, "263,000,000 hate messages and counting," *Countercurrents* (24 December 2021). Online: https://countercurrents.org/2021/12/263000000-hate-messages-and-counting/

6 Ibid.

7   Ibid.

8   Ibid.

9   Chris Hedges, "American commissars," *The Chris Hedges Report* (April 17, 2022). Online: https://chrishedges.substack.com/p/american-commissars?token=eyJ1c2VyX2lkIjo3MDAzNDAsIn Bvc3RfaWQiOjUyMzc0OTMzLCJfIjoiM0lYaW8iLCJpYXQi OjE2NTAyMzM2NzYsImV4cCI6MTY1MDIzNzI3NiwiaXNz IjoicHViLTc3ODg1MSIsInN1YiI6InBvc3QtcmVhY3Rpb24ifQ. pAX3hfu-DOficlT_rkSZSQfbfyS2Ppwgtgu9rvNvL6M&s=r

10 Ibid.

11 David M. Berry, *Critical Theory and the Digital* (London: Bloomsbury, 2014).

12 Goldberg, *Dread*, pp. 183–184.

13 Stuart J. Murray, "The suicidal state: In advance of an American requiem," *Philosophy & Rhetoric* 53:3 (June 2020). Online: https://scholarlypublishingcollective.org/psup/p-n-r/article/53/3/299/200241/The-Suicidal-State-In-Advance-of-an-American

14 Michel Foucault, *Society Must Be Defended: Lectures at the Collège de France, 1975–1976*, trans. David Macey (New York: Picador, 2003), p. 260.

15 Jeffrey Edward Green, *The Eyes of the People: Democracy in an Age of Spectatorship* (New York: Oxford University Press, 2011).

16 Hannah Arendt, "Lying in politics: Reflections on the Pentagon Papers," *The New York Review of Books* (18 November 1971). Online: https://www.nybooks.com/articles/1971/11/18/lying-in-politics-reflections-on-the-pentagon-pape/

17 Kiara Alfonseca, "Critical race theory in the classroom: Understanding the debate," *ABC News* (19 May 2021). Online: https://abcnews.go.com/US/critical-race-theory-classroom-understanding-debate/story?id=77627465

18 Ibid.

19 Arendt, "Lying in politics." Online: https://www.nybooks.com/articles/1971/11/18/lying-in-politics-reflections-on-the-pentagon-pape/

20 Ibid.

21 Ibid.

22 Steven Monacelli, "Confederate flags, conspiracies, and the ghost of JFK Jr.: What I saw at Trump's bananas Texas rally," *Rolling Stone* (20 January 2022). Online: https://www.rollingstone.com/politics/politics-features/trump-texas-rally-conspiracies-ghost-of-jfk-jr-1292592/

23   Peter Wade, "Newt Gingrich, who is advising GOP leadership, floats jail time for Jan. 6 committee members," *Rolling Stone* (23 January 2022). Online: https://www.rollingstone.com/politics/politics-news/gingrich-jan-6-committee-jail-1289408/

24   Jordan Levin, "Neo-Nazi demonstrations in Orlando mar Holocaust Remembrance Day," *Forward* (31 January 2022). Online: https://forward.com/news/481765/neo-nazi-demonstrations-in-orlando-mar-holocaust-remembrance-day/

Chapter 10

1   Cited in Edward Keenan, "Could the United States really be on the brink of another civil war?" *The Washington Post* (January 9, 2022). Online: https://www.stcatharinesstandard.ca/ts/news/world/2022/01/09/could-the-united-states-really-be-on-the-brink-of-another-civil-war.html

2   Joshua Sperling cited in Lisa Appignanesi, "Berger's way of being," *The New York Review of Books* (May 9, 2019). Online: https://www.nybooks.com/articles/2019/05/09/john-berger-ways-of-being/

3   Theodor W. Adorno, *Aspects of the New Right-Wing Extremism* (London: Polity, 2020), p. 10.

4   Alberto Toscano, "The long shadow of racial fascism," *Boston Review*. (October 27, 2020). Online http://bostonreview.net/race-politics/alberto-toscano-long-shadow-racial-fascism

5   Noam Chomsky, "Noam Chomsky: GOP's soft coup is still underway one year after Capitol assault," *Truthout* (January 6, 2022). Online: https://truthout.org/articles/noam-chomsky-gops-soft-coup-is-still-underway-one-year-after-capitol-assault/

6   Sarah Churchwell, "American fascism: It has happened again," *The New York Review of Books* (May 26, 2020).Online https://www.nybooks.com/daily/2020/06/22/american-fascism-it-has-happened-here/

7   Coco Das, "What are you going to do about the Nazi problem?" *refusefascism.org*. (November 24, 2020). Online: https://revcom.us/a/675/refuse-fascism-what-are-you-going-to-do-about-the-nazi-problem-en.html

8   See, for instance, Anthony DiMaggio, *Rising Fascism in America: It Can Happen Here* (New York: Routledge, 2022); Paul Street, *This Happened Here* (New York: Routledge, 2022); Ruth Ben-Ghiat,

Strongmen (New York: Norton, 2020); Bill V. Mullen and Christopher Vials, eds., *The U.S. Anti-Fascism Reader* (New York: Verso, 2020); Timothy Snyder, *On Tyranny: Twenty Lessons from the Twentieth Century* (New York: Tim Duggan Books, 2017); Jason Stanley, *How Fascism Works* (New York: Random House, 2018); Henry A. Giroux, *American Nightmare: Facing the Challenge of Fascism* (San Francisco: City Lights Books, 2018); Carl Boggs, *Fascism Old and New* (New York: Routledge, 2018).

9   Cleve R. Wootson Jr., "Trump and allies try to redefine racism by casting White men as victims," *The Washington Post* (February 5, 2022). Online: https://www.washingtonpost.com/politics/2022/02/05/trump-redefine-racism/

10 Cited in Vassilis Rafalidis, "How to become a good Nazi," *Praxis Review* (September 14, 2026). Online: https://praxisreview.gr/%ce%b2-%cf%81%ce%b1%cf%86%ce%b1%ce%b7%ce%bb%ce%af%ce%b4%ce%b7%cf%82-%cf%80%cf%8e%cf%82-%ce%b8%ce%b1-%ce%b3%ce%af%ce%bd%ce%b5%ce%b9%cf%82-%ce%a-d%ce%bd%ce%b1%cf%82-%ce%ba%ce%b1%ce%bb%cf%8c/

11 Umberto Eco made this clear in a brilliant essay: "Ur-fascism," *The New York Review of Books* (June 22, 1995). Online: http://www.nybooks.com/articles/1995/06/22/ur-fascism/?pagination=false&printpage=true

12 Lawrence Eppard and Henry Giroux, *Inequality and Freedom* (New York: Oxford University Press, 2022).

13 Peter Dolack, "As long as capitalism exists, the threat of fascism exists," *Counterpunch* (January 16, 2022). Online: https://www.counterpunch.org/2022/01/16/as-long-as-capitalism-exists-the-threat-of-fascism-exists/

14 A number of conservatives, journalists, scholars, and pundits support the notion that the United States when it comes to the slide into authoritarianism may well be past the point of no return. See, for instance, a summary of these positions in Thomas B. Edsall, "How to tell when your country is past the point of no return," *New York Times* (December 15, 2021). Online: https://www.nytimes.com/2021/12/15/opinion/republicans-democracy-minority-rule.html

15 These issues are discussed in great detail in the invaluable book by Roberto J. Gonzalez, Hugh Gusterson, and Gustaaf Houtman, eds., *Militarization: A Reader* (Durham, NC: Duke University Press, 2019).

16 Julia Jacobo, "This is what Trump told supporters before many stormed Capitol Hill," *ABC News* (January 7, 2021). Online: https://abcnews.go.com/Politics/trump-told-supporters-stormed-capitol-hill/story?id=75110558

17 Paul Krugman, "Appeasement got us where we are," *New York Times* (January 7, 2021). Online: https://www.nytimes.com/2021/01/07/opinion/donald-trump-fascism.html

18 One prominent example appeared in an issue of Vox. Dylan Mathews, "Is Trump a fascist? 8 experts weigh in," *Vox* (October 23, 2021). Online: https://www.vox.com/policy-and-politics/21521958/what-is-fascism-signs-donald-trump. Ignored in this piece was the crucial work of historians such as Jason Stanley, Timothy Snyder, Sarah Churchill, and Ruth Ben-Ghiat.

19 Laurence H. Tribe, "The risk of a coup in the next US election is greater now than it ever was under Trump," *The Guardian* (January 3, 2022). Online: https://www.theguardian.com/commentisfree/2022/jan/03/risk-us-coup-next-us-election-greater-than-under-trump

20 See Paul Krugman, "Why did Republicans become so extreme?," *New York Times* (June 28, 2022). Online: https://www.nytimes.com/2022/06/27/opinion/republicans-extreme-abortion.html; Francine Prose, "We Americans are dancing on the Titanic. Our iceberg is not far away," *The Guardian* (June 27, 2022). Online: https://www.theguardian.com/commentisfree/2022/jun/27/we-americans-are-dancing-on-the-titanic-our-iceberg-is-not-far-away

Chapter 11

1 Jonathan Crary, *Scorched Earth: Beyond the Digital Age to a Post-Capitalist World* (London: Verso, 2022), p. 2.

2 Toni Morrison, "Racism and Fascism," *The Journal of Negro Education* (Summer 1995), pp. 384–385. Online: https://www.leeannhunter.com/gender/wp-content/uploads/2012/11/Morrison-article.pdf

3 Ibid.

4 Ibid.

5 C. Wright Mills, "The Cultural Apparatus," *The Politics of Truth: Selected Writings of C. Wright Mills* (Oxford University Press, 2008), pp. 203–212

6 Raymond Williams, *Communications* (New York: Barnes & Noble, 1967), p. 15.

7   Wright Mills, "The Cultural Apparatus," p. 204.

8   Ibid., p. 205.

9   Ibid., p. 204.

10 Of course, the political centrality of culture and power has long been a central concern of critical theory and cultural studies, especially in the work of the Frankfurt School, Raymond Williams, Stuart Hall, Lawrence Grossberg, and others.

11 Jonathan Crary, 24/7 (London: Verso 2013).

12 For an updated treatment of this issue, see Noam Chomsky and Marv Waterstone, *Consequences of Capitalism* (Chicago: Haymarket Books, 2021).

13 Stuart Hall and Alan O'Shea, "The danger of common sense," *OpenDemocracy* (November 3, 2013). Online: https://www.opendemocracy.net/en/opendemocracyuk/danger-of-common-sense/

14 Raymond Williams, *Communications* (New York: Barnes & Noble, 1967), p. 15.

15 On this issue, see the brilliant work of Kenneth Saltman and Nicole Nguyen, eds., *Handbook of Critical Approaches to Politics and Policy of Education* (New York: Routledge, 2022); Kenneth Saltman, *The Politics of Education*, second edition (New York: Routledge, 2018); Donaldo Macedo and Inny Accioly, eds., *Education, Equality and Justice in the New Normal: Global Responses to the Pandemic* (London: Bloomsbury, 2021).

16 bell hooks, *Teaching to Transgress* (New York: Routledge, 1994), p. 4.

17 Larry Grossberg, "Introduction: Bringin' it all back home-pedagogy in cultural studies," in Henry A. Giroux and Peter McLaren, eds., *Between Borders: Pedagogy and the Politics of Cultural Studies* (New York: Routledge, 1994), p. 29.

18 I have taken this issue up in a number of books, see Henry A. Giroux, *Pedagogy of Resistance: Against Manufactured Ignorance* (London: Bloomsbury, 2022).

19 Richard D. Wolff, "U.S. Politicians spend their time papering over the social problems caused by profit-driven capitalism," *CounterPunch* (January 31, 2022). Online: https://www.counterpunch.org/2022/01/31/u-s-politicians-spend-their-time-papering-over-the-social-problems-caused-by-profit-driven-capitalism/

20 Evan Osnos, "Dan Bongino and the big business of returning Trump to power," *The New Yorker* (December 27, 2021). Online: https://www.newyorker.com/magazine/2022/01/03/dan-bongino-and-the-big-business-of-returning-trump-to-power

21 Paul Matzko, "Talk radio is turning millions of Americans into conservatives," *New York Times* (October 9, 2020). Online: https://www.nytimes.com/2020/10/09/opinion/talk-radio-conservatives-trumpism.html; see also, Paul Matzko, *The Radio Right: How a Band of Broadcasters Took on the Federal Government and Built the Modern Conservative Movement* (New York: Oxford University Press, 2020).

22 Osnos, "Dan Bongino." Online: https://www.newyorker.com/magazine/2022/01/03/dan-bongino-and-the-big-business-of-returning-trump-to-power

23 Ibid.

24 Richard L. Hansen, *Cheap Speech: How Disinformation Poisons Our Politics—and How to Cure It* (New Haven, CT: Yale University Press, 2022); Nicole Hemmer, *Messengers of the Right: Conservative Media and the Transformation of American Politics* (Philadelphia: University of Pennsylvania, 2018).

25 Paul Gilroy, "British Cultural Studies and the Pitfalls of Identity," in Houston Baker, Jr., Manthia Diawara, and Ruth Lindeborg, eds., *Black British Cultural Studies* (Chicago: University of Chicago Press, 1996), p. 225.

26 Ibid.

Chapter 12

1 David Harvey, "Neoliberalism is a political project." *Jacobin*, [07.23.2016]. Online: https://www.jacobinmag.com/2016/07/david-harvey-neoliberalism-capitalism-labor-crisis-resistance/

2 Robin D. G. Kelley, "Sorry, not sorry," *Boston Review* (September 13, 2018) Online: http://bostonreview.net/race-literature-culture/robin-d-g-kelley-sorry-not-sorry

3 Jonathan Crary, *Scorched Earth: Beyond the Digital Age to a Post-Capitalist World* (London: Verso, 2022), p. 11.

4 Paul Waldman, "Republicans are waging a war on schools. When will Democrats fight back?" *The Washington Post* (January 10, 2022). Online: https://www.washingtonpost.com/opinions/2022/01/10/republican-war-on-schools/

5 Elizabeth A. Harris and Alexandra Alter, "Book banning efforts surged in 2021. These titles were the most targeted," *New York Times* (April 4, 2022). Online: https://www.nytimes.com/2022/04/04/books/banned-books-libraries.html?referringSource=articleShare

6   Ibid.

7   Greg Sargent, "A GOP proposal targeting 'negative' U.S. history is cause for renewed alarm," *The Washington Post* (January 31, 2022). Online: https://www.washingtonpost.com/opinions/2022/01/31/gop-proposal-targets-negative-us-history/

8   Ibid.

9   Bess Levin, "Virginia governor urges parents to rat out schools for teaching kids about 'divisive' topics like racism," *Vanity Fair* (January 25, 2022). Online: https://www.vanityfair.com/news/2022/01/glenn-youngkin-virginia-parents-tip-line

10 Jeffrey Sachs, "Steep rise in gag orders, many sloppily drafted," *Pen America* (January 24, 2022). Online: https://pen.org/steep-rise-gag-orders-many-sloppily-drafted/

11 Chris Walker, "Iowa Republican authors bill demanding cameras in every classroom in state," *Truthout* (February 4, 2022). Online: https://truthout.org/articles/iowa-republican-authors-bill-demanding-cameras-in-every-classroom-in-state/

12 Ibid.

13 Ibid.

14 Guenter Lewy, *Harmful and Undesirable: Book Censorship in Nazi Germany* (London: Oxford University Press, 2016).

15 John Simkin, "Education in Nazi Germany," *Spartacus Educational* (2021). Online: https://spartacus-educational.com/GEReducation.htm

16 See, for instance, Victor Klemperer, *The Language of the Third Reich* (London: Bloomsbury, 2006).

17 Joel McNally, "Republican attacks on public schools never die," *Shepherd Express* (February 7, 2022). Online: https://shepherdexpress.com/news/taking-liberties/republican-attacks-on-public-schools-never-die/. The underlying factors at work in the right-wing attempt to destroy public education are also clear in Barbara Milner, "Why the right hates public education," *Rethinking Schools* (Summer 2002). Online: https://rethinkingschools.org/special-collections/why-the-right-hates-public-education/

18 bell hooks, *Teaching Critical Thinking* (New York: Routledge, 2009), p. 17.

19 George Packer, "The grown-ups are losing it," *The Atlantic* (March 10, 2022). Online: https://www.theatlantic.com/magazine/archive/2022/04/pandemic-politics-public-schools/622824/

20 The literature on the politics of education is too enormous to cite and extends from seminal work by John Dewey, Paulo Freire, Herbert

Gintis, and Sam Bowles to Ivan Illich, myself, Kenneth Saltman, and Peter McLaren.

21 Peter Fleming, *Dark Academia: How Universities Die* (London: Pluto, 2021), p. 53.

22 Stanley Fish, "On balance," *The Chronicle of Higher Education* (April 1, 2005). Online: https://www.chronicle.com/article/on-balance/

23 Jamelle Bouie, "You just can't tell the truth about America anymore," *New York Times* (February 18, 2022). Online: https://www.nytimes.com/2022/02/18/opinion/us-history-censorship.html

24 Ibid.

25 Andrew O'Hehir, "Legendary reporter Carl Bernstein on journalism, Trump and history: 'The truth is not neutral'," *Salon* (February 1, 2022). Online: https://www.salon.com/2022/02/01/legendary-newsman-carl-bernstein-on-journalism-and-history-the-truth-is-not-neutral/

26 Laura Meckler and Hannah Natanson, "New critical race theory laws have teachers scared, confused and self-censoring," *The Washington Post* (February 14, 2022). Online: https://www.washingtonpost.com/education/2022/02/14/critical-race-theory-teachers-fear-laws/

27 Amanda Marcotte, "Republicans' war on education is the most crucial part of their push for fascism," *Salon* (December 21, 2021). Online: https://www.salon.com/2021/12/02/republicans-on-education-is-the-most-crucial-part-of-their-push-for-fascism/

28 Kyle Stucker, "Attacks against teaching the history of enslaved Africans and their descendants in America," *USA Today* (June 14, 2022). Online: https://www.usatoday.com/story/news/2022/06/15/which-states-celebrate-juneteenth-ban-critical-race-theory-slavery-racism/9617749002/

29 Ibid.

30 Cited in Nick Anderson and Susan Svrluga, "College faculty are fighting back against state bills on critical race theory," *The Washington Post* (February 19, 2022). Online: https://www.washingtonpost.com/education/2022/02/19/colleges-critical-race-theory-bills/

31 See, for instance, Richard M. Fried, *Nightmare in Red: The McCarthy Era in Perspective* (London: Oxford University Press, 1991); M. Stanton Evans, *Blacklisted by History: The Untold Story of Joe McCarthy* (New York: Crown, 2007), and Larry Tye,

Demagogue: The Life and Long Shadow of Senator Joe McCarthy (New York: Mariner Books, 2020).

32 David Badash, "'TV terrorist' Donald Trump blasted for telling followers they 'must lay down their very lives' to defend against CRT," Alternet (March 13, 2022). Online: https://www.alternet.org/2022/03/trump/

33 Jonathan Friedman and James Tager, *Educational Gag Orders* (New York: PEN America, 2021). Online: https://pen.org/report/educational-gag-orders/#

34 Francine Prose, "Texas schools are being told to teach opposing views of the Holocaust. Why?" *The Guardian* (October 19, 2021). Online: https://www.theguardian.com/commentisfree/2021/oct/19/texas-holocaust-curriculum-schools-hb-3979

35 Judd Legum, "'Moms For Liberty' says book about MLK violates new law banning CRT in Tennessee," *Popular Information* (December 1, 2021). Online: https://popular.info/p/moms-for-liberty-says-book-about

36 Ruth Ben-Ghiat, "One year of Lucid: Tracking authoritarianism, democratic decline, and resistance," *Lucid* (March 12, 2022). Online: https://lucid.substack.com/p/one-year-of-lucid-tracking-authoritarianism?s=r

37 Legum, "'Moms For Liberty'."

38 Ibid.

39 Ibid.

40 Ibid.

41 Kathryn Joyce, "Fighting back against CRT panic: Educators organize around the threat to academic freedom," *Salon* (March 7, 2022). Online: https://www.salon.com/2022/03/07/fighting-back-against-crt-panic-educators-organize-around-the-to-academic-freedom/

42 Ibid.

43 Angela Y. Davis, *Freedom Is a Constant Struggle: Ferguson, Palestine and the Foundations of a Movement*, ed. Frank Barat. (Chicago: Haymarket Books, 2016), pp. 65–66.

44 It should be noted that bell hooks was a pioneer in connecting critical pedagogy to a critique of sexism and bourgeois white feminism. See, especially, bell hooks, *Teaching to Transgress: Education as the Practice of Freedom* (New York: Routledge, 1994); bell hooks, *Teaching Critical Thinking: Practical Wisdom* (New York: Routledge, 2009); bell hooks, *Isn't I a Woman: Black Women*

and Feminism, second edition (New York: Routledge, 2014). Second-generation work connecting critical pedagogy to gender and race issues can be found in Antonia Darder, *Culture and Power in the Classroom: Educational Foundations for the Schooling of Bicultural Students* (New York: Routledge, 2012); Antonia Darder, *Reinventing Paulo Freire: A Pedagogy of Love* (New York: Routledge, 2017); Antonia Darder, *A Dissident Voice* (New York: Peter Lang, 2011).

Chapter 13

1   Cornelius Castoriadis, "Democracy as procedure and democracy as regime," *Constellations* 4:1 (1997), p. 5.

2   See Seth Adler, "By party or by formation," *The Bullet* (June 27, 2018); also see the important work of the late Stanley Aronowitz, especially his *Left Turn: Forging a New Political Future* (New York: Routledge, 2006).

3   Amy Goodman, "Angela Davis on imagining new worlds, the campaign to free Mumia and the Biden presidency," *Democracy Now* (December 28, 2021). Online: https://www.democracynow.org/2021/12/28/angela_davis_25th_anniversary_taped_segment_part

4   Gayatri Chakravorty Spivak, *Can the Subaltern Speak?* (Cambridge: Afterall Books, 2021).

5   Slavoj Žižek, *Demanding the Impossible*, ed. Yong-June Park (Cambridge: Polity Press, 2013), p. 79.

6   Hannah Arendt, *The Origins of Totalitarianism* (New York: Houghton Mifflin Harcourt, 2001). p. 474.

7   Anne Applebaum, "Why we should read Hannah Arendt now," *The Atlantic* (March 17, 2022). Online: https://www.anneapplebaum.com/2022/03/17/why-we-should-read-hannah-arendt-now/

8   Liz Theoharis, "Inequality and the coronavirus," *Tom Dispatch* (April 21, 2020). Online http://www.tomdispatch.com/post/176691/tomgram%3A_liz_theoharis%2C_circling_the_ruins/

9   See Edgar Cabanas and Eva Illouz, *Manufacturing Happy Citizens* (London: Polity, 2019).

10 John Steppling, "To Catch the Exception," in *John Steppling: The Practice of Writing* (April 16, 2022). Online:https://john-steppling.com/2022/04/to-catch-the-exception/

11 Cited in George Yancy: "Bodies without Edges: Rethinking Borders of Invulnerability," in Brad Evans, ed. *The Quarantine Files*

(Los Angeles: Los Angeles Review of Books, 2020), Online: https://
lareviewofbooks.org/article/quarantine-files-thinkers-self-isolation/?fb
clid=IwAR3VDovJfePU7AaIW6o0BQ5jZvLFoqdbQ7tS4jGXLY6Cd
mU4VmHbHz-Km-o

12 Anne Applebaum, "There is no liberal world order," *The Atlantic*
(March 31, 2022). Online: https://www.theatlantic.com/magazine/
archive/2022/05/autocracy-could-destroy-democracy-russia-
ukraine/629363/

13 Ibid.

14 Ibid.

Chapter 14

1 Maya Schenwar, "Angela Davis, Gina Dent, Erica Meiners and
Beth Richie talk abolition feminism," *Truthout* (February 7, 2022).
Online: https://truthout.org/articles/angela-davis-gina-dent-erica-
meiners-and-beth-richie-talk-abolition-feminism/

2 Anthony DiMaggio, "The limits of #MeToo: Sectionalism,
economism, and 'identity politics' on the left," *CounterPunch*
(February 5, 2021). Online: https://www.counterpunch.org/2018/02/05/
the-limits-of-metoo-sectionalism-economism-and-identity-politics-on-
the-left/

3 Rafael Khachaturian and Sean Guillory, "The American left
resurgent: Prospects and tensions," *Socialist Project: The Bullet*
(February 7, 2019). Online: https://socialistproject.ca/2019/02/the-
american-left-resurgent/

4 See on this issue, Nelson George's erudite discussion of Angela
Davis's work, i.e., Nelson George, "Angela Davis," *New York Times
Style Magazine* (October 19, 2020). Online: https://www.nytimes.
com/interactive/2020/10/19/t-magazine/angela-davis.html

5 Sam Gindin, "The organizing challenge and American capitalism,"
The Socialist Project (July 20, 2021). Online: https://socialistproject.
ca/2021/07/organizing-challenge-and-american-capitalism/

6 E. Tammy Kim, "Do today's unions have a fighting chance against
corporate America?" *The New York Times Magazine* (February 17,
2022). Online: https://www.nytimes.com/2022/02/17/magazine/
unions-amazon.html

7 Gindin, "Organizing challenge."

8   Karen Weise and Noam Scheiber, "Amazon workers on Staten Island vote to unionize in stunning win for labor," *New York Times* (April 1, 2022). Online: https://www.nytimes.com/2022/04/01/technology/amazon-union-staten-island.html

9   Chris Hedges is instructive here. See Chris Hedges, "Mass politics must be rooted in class struggle," *The Real News* (January 25, 2022). Online: https://therealnews.com/chris-hedges-mass-politics-must-be-rooted-in-class-struggle

10   Daniella Silva, "Minneapolis teachers strike continues as union and district remain far apart on deal," NBC News (March 10, 2022). Online: https://www.nbcnews.com/news/us-news/minneapolis-teachers-strike-continues-union-district-remain-far-apart-rcna19573

11   Emily Tate, "Our nation's teachers are hustling to survive," *EdSurge* (March 30, 2022). Online: https://www.edsurge.com/news/2022-03-30-our-nation-s-teachers-are-hustling-to-survive

12   Ibid.

13   See the list of oppositional movements opposing this frontal assault by Republicans provided by Jeremy Mohler in "School culture wars are distracting us from something remarkable happening." *In the Public Interest* (March 24, 2022). Online: https://mail.google.com/mail/u/0/#inbox/WhctKKXPknxfNlJTDznxXzDlsbhscWckNjctB WhpgwNpfQprKKBmzZxccKXLWqCVHjTskjB

14   Alex Woodward, "Disney workers stage daily walkouts to protest 'Don't say gay' and demand protections for LGBT+ staff," *Independent* (March 17, 2022). Online: https://www.independent.co.uk/news/world/americas/us-politics/disney-employees-walkout-dont-say-gay-b2037581.html?amp

15   Gindin, "Organizing challenge."

16   On this issue, see Joe Burns, *Class Struggle Unionism* (Chicago: Haymarket, 2022). Also, see the excellent work by Michael Yates, especially *Work Work Work: Labor, Alienation, and Class Struggle* (New York: Monthly Review Press, 2022) and Michael D. Yates, *Can the Working Class Change the World?* (New York: Monthly Review Press, 2018).

17   Nancy Fraser, "Is capitalism necessary," *Politics/Letters* (May 20, 2019). Online: http://quarterly.politicsslashletters.org/is-capitalism-necessarily-racist/

18   Robin D. G. Kelley cited in Amy Goodman, "Historian Robin D. G. Kelley: Years of racial justice organizing laid groundwork for today's uprising," *Democracy Now!* (June 11, 2020). Online: https://www.democracynow.org/2020/6/11/robin_dg_kelley_social_movements

19 Martin Luther King, Jr, "Beyond Vietnam—A time to break silence," *American Rhetoric*. Speech Delivered April 4, 1967, at the Riverside Church, New York City. Online: https://www.americanrhetoric.com/speeches/mlkatimetobreaksilence.htm

20 Ernst Bloch, "Something's missing: A discussion between Ernst Bloch and Theodor W. Adorno on the contradictions of utopian longing." In Ernst Bloch, *The Utopian Function of Art and Literature: Selected Essays* (Cambridge, MA: MIT Press, 1988), pp. 3–4.

21 Joao Biehl, *Life in the Zone of Social Abandonment* (New Haven, CT: Yale, 2006), p. 155.

22 Ben Davis, *Art in the After-Culture* (Chicago: Haymarket Press, 2022).

Chapter 15

1 David Frum, "Vaccinated America has had enough," *The Atlantic* (July 23, 2021) Online: https://www.theatlantic.com/ideas/archive/2021/07/vaccinated-america-breaking-point-anti-vaxxers/619539/

2 Paul Krugman, "When 'freedom' means the right to destroy," *New York Times* (February 15, 2022). Online: https://www.nytimes.com/2022/02/14/opinion/canada-protests-black-lives-matter.html

3 Chris Walker, "Far right truckers in 'Freedom Convoy' stopped by Ottawa neighborhood residents," *Truthout* (February 16, 2022). Online: https://truthout.org/articles/far-right-truckers-in-freedom-convoy-stopped-by-ottawa-neighborhood-residents/

4 Ibid.

5 Press Release, "Teamsters denounce freedom convoy blockade at Canadian border," *International Brotherhood of Teamsters* (February 10, 2022). Online: https://teamster.org/2022/02/teamsters-denounce-freedom-convoy-blockade-at-canadian-border/

6 Rachel Aiello, "Trudeau makes history, invokes Emergencies Act to address trucker protests," *CTV News* (February 14, 2022). Online: https://www.ctvnews.ca/politics/trudeau-makes-history-invokes-emergencies-act-to-address-trucker-protests-1.5780283

7 Emily Leedham, "Canada's 'Freedom convoy' is a front for a right-wing, anti-worker agenda," *Jacobin* (February 5, 2022). Online: https://jacobinmag.com/2022/02/canada-freedom-convoy-conservative-right-wing-anti-worker-anti-vaccine

8 Rupert Neate, "Elon Musk criticized for likening Justin Trudeau to Adolf Hitler in tweet," *The Guardian* (February 17, 2022).

Online: https://www.theguardian.com/technology/2022/feb/17/elon-musk-criticised-for-comparing-justin-trudeau-to-adolf-hitler-tweet-auschwitz

9   Timothy Bella, "Rand Paul urges truckers to disrupt Super Bowl and come to D.C.: 'I hope they clog up cities'," *The Washington Post* (February 12, 2022). Online: https://www.washingtonpost.com/politics/2022/02/12/rand-paul-trucker-protest-super-bowl/

10 Ibid.

11 Justin Ling, "5G and QAnon: How conspiracy theorists steered Canada's anti-vaccine trucker protest," *The Guardian* (February 8, 2022). Online: https://www.theguardian.com/world/2022/feb/08/canada-ottawa-trucker-protest-extremist-qanon-neo-nazi

12 Ruth Ben-Ghiat, "Extremism expert Stephanie Carvin on the convoys and how to respond to them," *Lucid* (February 16, 2022). Online: https://lucid.substack.com/p/extremism-expert-stephanie-carvin?r=f0dw

13 Ibid.

14 Ling, "5G and QAnon."

15 Leedham, "Canada's 'Freedom convoy'." Online: https://jacobinmag.com/2022/02/canada-freedom-convoy-conservative-right-wing-anti-worker-anti-vaccine

16 Kayla Preston, "'Freedom convoy' rolls through Ottawa encouraging the participation of Canada's far-right," *The Conversation* (February 1, 2022). Online: https://theconversation.com/freedom-convoy-rolls-through-ottawa-encouraging-the-participation-of-canadas-far-right-175902

17 Ibid.

18 Al Jazeera staff, "Canada's NDP leader says trucker convoy aims to 'overthrow' gov't," *Al-Jazeera* (February 7, 2022). Online: https://www.aljazeera.com/news/2022/2/7/canada-ndp-leader-trucker-convoy-aims-to-overthrow-govt

19 Sarah Turnbull, "Feds ready to act should 'foul play' be detected in trucker convoy funding, says public safety minister," *CTV News* (February 7, 2022). Online: https://www.ctvnews.ca/politics/feds-ready-to-act-should-foul-play-be-detected-in-trucker-convoy-funding-says-public-safety-minister-1.5771551

20 Aaron C. Davis, Andrew Ba Tran, and Dalton Bennett, "Which U.S. communities sent money to support the Canadian trucker protests?" *The Washington Post* (February 15, 2022). Online: https://www.washingtonpost.com/investigations/2022/02/15/american-donors-freedom-convoy-zipcodes/

21 Jon Woodward, "Anonymous donations to convoy as high as $215,000 concern Canadian MPs," *CTV News* (February 11, 2022). Online: https://toronto.ctvnews.ca/anonymous-donations-to-convoy-as-high-as-215-000-concern-canadian-mps-1.5777497

22 The Canadian Press, "NDP want U.S. ambassador to testify about American funding of Ottawa protests," *Trial Times* (February 10, 2022). Online: https://www.trailtimes.ca/news/ndp-want-u-s-ambassador-to-testify-about-american-funding-of-ottawa-protests/

23 Al Jazeera staff, "Canada's NDP leader." Online: https://www.aljazeera.com/news/2022/2/7/canada-ndp-leader-trucker-convoy-aims-to-overthrow-govt

24 Leedham, "Canada's 'Freedom convoy'." Online: https://jacobinmag.com/2022/02/canada-freedom-convoy-conservative-right-wing-anti-worker-anti-vaccine

25 Ibid.

26 On the truckers move into the United States, see Steve O'Keefe, "Who's behind the people's convoy to Washington DC?" *Counterpunch* (February 21, 2022). Online: https://www.counterpunch.org/2022/02/21/whos-behind-the-peoples-convoy-to-washington-dc/

27 Elisabeth Anker, "The exploitation of 'freedom' in America," *New York Times* (February 4, 2022). Online: https://www.nytimes.com/2022/02/04/opinion/ugly-freedom-discrimination-racism-sexism.html

28 Ibid.

29 Zygmunt Bauman, *Liquid Times: Living in the Age of Uncertainty* (London: Polity Press, 2007), p. 14.

30 Magdi Semrau, "Why anti-vaxx attitudes fit so perfectly with far-right ideology across the globe," *AlterNet* (August 20, 2021). Online: https://www.alternet.org/2021/08/right-wing-anti-vaxx/

31 Ruth Ben-Ghiat, "Vaccine scientist Peter Hotez on anti-science aggression," *Lucid* (November 17, 2021). Online: https://lucid.substack.com/p/vaccine-scientist-peter-hotez-on

32 Ibid.

33 Dennis Wagner, "The COVID culture war: At what point should personal freedom yield to the common good?" *USA Today* (August 2, 2021). Online: https://www.usatoday.com/story/news/nation/2021/08/02/covid-culture-war-masks-vaccine-pits-liberty-against-common-good/5432614001/

34 This issue is extensively explored in Lawrence Eppard and Henry A. Giroux, *On Inequality and Freedom* (New York: Oxford University Press, 2022).

35 Press Release, "Ten richest men double their fortunes in pandemic while incomes of 99 percent of humanity fall," *Oxfam International* (January 17, 2022). Online: https://www.oxfam.org/en/press-releases/ten-richest-men-double-their-fortunes-pandemic-while-incomes-99-percent-humanity

36 Ronald Aronson, *We: Reviving Social Hope* (Chicago: The University of Chicago Press, 2017), P. 143.

37 Erich Fromm, *On Disobedience: Why Freedom Means Saying "No" to Power* (New York: Harper Perennial Modern Thought Press, 2010), P. 69.

38 Jessica Corbett, "UN expert warns of near 'tyranny' against voting rights of U.S. minorities amid GOP attacks," *Salon* (November 25, 2021). Online: https://www.salon.com/2021/11/25/un-expert-warns-of-near-tyranny-against-voting-rights-of-us-minorities-amid_partner/

39 Agence France-Presse in Stockholm, "US added to list of 'backsliding' democracies for first time," *The Guardian* (November 22, 2021). Online: https://www.theguardian.com/us-news/2021/nov/22/us-list-backsliding-democracies-civil-liberties-international; Ishaan Tharoor, "Democracy is in decline around the world—and Trump is part of the problem," Washington Post (March 5, 2020). Online https://www.washingtonpost.com/world/2020/03/05/democracy-is-decline-around-world-trump-is-part-problem/; see also Yascha Mounk, "Dictators Aren't Pretending Anymore," *The Atlantic* (February 24, 2022). Online: https://www.theatlantic.com/ideas/archive/2022/02/democracy-crisis-autocrat-rise-putin/622895/?utm_source=newsletter&utm_medium=email&utm_campaign=atlantic-daily-newsletter&utm_content=20220225&utm_term=The%20Atlantic%20Daily

Chapter 16

1 Antonio Gramsci, English translation, *Selections from the Prison Notebooks*, "Wave of Materialism" and "Crisis of Authority" (New York: International Publishers, 1971), pp. 275–276.

2 James Meeks, "What are you willing to do?," *London Review of Books* (May 26, 2022), p. 3.

3 A conversation between Lani Guinier and Anna Deavere Smith, "Rethinking power, rethinking theater," *Theater* 31: 3 (Winter 2002), pp. 34–35. ADVANCE \d 12

4 William Deresiewicz, *Excellent Sheep: The Miseducation of the American Elite* (New York: Free Press, 2014).

5 McKay Coppins, "A secretive hedge fund is gutting newsrooms," *The Atlantic* (October 14, 2021). Online: https://www.theatlantic.com/magazine/archive/2021/11/alden-global-capital-killing-americas-newspapers/620171/

6 Amy Goodman, "Angela Davis speaks on abolition, justice for Palestine and critical race theory," *Truthout* (December 28, 2021). Online: https://truthout.org/video/angela-davis-speaks-on-abolition-justice-for-palestine-and-critical-race-theory/

7 Paul Gilroy, "The 2019 Holberg Lecture, by Laureate Paul Gilroy: Never again: refusing race and salvaging the human," *Holbergprisen* (November 11, 2019). Online: https://holbergprisen.no/en/news/holberg-prize/2019-holberg-lecture-laureate-paul-gilroy

8 Zygmunt Bauman and Keith Tester, *Conversations with Zygmunt Bauman* (London: Polity Press, 2001), p. 19.

9 Primo Levi, *In the Black Hole of Auschwitz*, trans. Sharon Wood (Cambridge: Polity Press, 1974, 2005), p. 34.

10 Cited in Leo Panitch and Sam Gindin, "Transcending Pessimism: Rekindling Socialist Imagination," in Leo Panitch and Sam Gindin, eds., *Necessary and Unnecessary Utopians* (New York: Monthly Review Press, 1999), p. 4.

Chapter 17

1 See, for instance, Nancy MacLean, *Democracy in Chains: The Deep History of the Radical Right's Stealth Plan for America* (New York: Viking, 2017).

2 Heather Cox Richardson, "Interview with President Biden," *Letters from an American* (March 4, 2022). Online: https://heathercoxrichardson.substack.com/p/interview-with-president-biden?s=r

3 Ernst Bloch, *Principle of Hope*, vol. 1 (Cambridge, MA: MIT Press, 1995), p. 7.

4   Anson Rabinach, "Unclaimed heritage: Ernst Bloch's heritage of
    our times and the theory of fascism," *New German Critique* (spring
    1977), p. 7.

5   Nina Turner, "Good ideas are not enough, we need to marry
    our ideas to power," *Jacobin* (March 16, 2021), Online: https://
    jacobinmag.com/2021/03/nina-turner-congress-progressive-policy

6   Editors, "Now what?" *Jacobin* (No. 24, winter 2017). Online: https://
    www.jacobinmag.com/2017/02/now-what

7   Robin D. G. Kelley, "Black study, black struggle," *Boston Review*
    (March 7, 2016). Online: https://bostonreview.net/forum/robin-d-g-
    kelley-black-study-black-struggle

8   I have examined this issue extensively in Henry A. Giroux,
    Neoliberalism's War on Higher Education, second edition (Chicago:
    Haymarket Press, 2010).

9   Henry A. Giroux, *University in Chains: Confronting the Military-
    Industrial-Academic Complex* (New York: Routledge, 2007); Daniel
    Golden, Spy *Schools: How the CIA, FBI, and Foreign Intelligence
    Secretly Exploit America's Universities* (New York: Henry Holt, 2017).

10 Paul Allen Miller, "Tyranny, Fear, and Parrhesia: Truth in the
    Neoliberal University, or 'How do I know I am not Heidegger?'"
    Symploke 29:2 (2021.)179–195.

11 Cited in Jennifer Ruth, "The increasingly authoritarian war on
    tenure," *The Chronicle of Higher Education* (February 23, 2022).
    Online: https://www.chronicle.com/article/the-increasingly-
    authoritarian-war-on-tenure?utm_source=Iterable&utm_
    medium=email&utm_campaign=campaign_3763729_nl_Afternoon-
    Update_date_20220223&cid=pm&source=ams&sourceid=&cid2=g
    en_login_refresh

12 Kathryn Joyce, "Fighting back against CRT panic: Educators organize
    around the threat to academic freedom," *Salon* (March 7, 2022).
    Online: https://www.salon.com/2022/03/07/fighting-back-against-crt-
    panic-educators-organize-around-the-to-academic-freedom/

13 There are too many notable sources to cite on this issue. Three
    important sources include Christopher Newfield, *Unmaking the
    Public University* (Cambridge, MA: Harvard University Press, 2008);
    Benjamin Ginsberg, *The Fall of the Faculty* (New York: Oxford
    University Press, 2011); Henry Heller, *The Capitalist University*
    (London: Pluto Press, 2016), and Lawrence Busch, *Knowledge for
    Sale: The Neoliberal Takeover of Higher Education* (Cambridge, MA:
    MIT Press, 2017).

14 The classic text on this issue is Bill Readings, *The University in Ruins* (Cambridge, MA: Harvard University Press, 1997). Also see Christopher Newfield, *Unmaking the Public University* (Cambridge, MA: Harvard University Press, 2008); Henry Heller, *The Capitalist University* (London: Pluto Press, 2016).

15 Giroux, *Neoliberalism's War*.

16 Kathryn Joyce, "Salon investigates: The war on public schools is being fought from Hillsdale College," *Salon* (March 16, 2022). Online: https://www.salon.com/2022/03/16/salon-investigates-the-on-public-schools-is-being-fought-from-hillsdale-college/

17 Ariel Dorfman, "Defying fear in traumatic times," *Counterpunch* (November 11, 2020). Online: https://www.counterpunch.org/2020/11/11/defying-fear-in-traumatic-times/

18 Pierre Bourdieu and Gunter Grass, "A Literature From Below," *The Nation* (July 3, 2000), p. 25.

19 Henry A. Giroux, *Race, Politics, and Pandemic Pedagogy: Education in a Time of Crisis* (London: Bloomsbury, 2021).

20 Jean Seaton, "Why Orwell's 1984 could be about now," BBC (May 7, 2018). https://www.bbc.com/culture/article/20180507-why-orwells-1984-could-be-about-now

21 Pierre Bourdieu and Gunter Grass, "The 'progressive' restoration: A Franco-German dialogue," *New Left Review* 14 (March–April 2002), pp. 63–64.

22 Arunhdhati Roy, *Power Politics* (Cambridge, MA: South End Press, 2001), p. 3.

23 Stuart Hall, *Writings on Media*, ed. Charlotte Brundson (Durham, NC: Duke University Press, 2021), p. 112.

Chapter 18

1 Ben Davis, *Art in the After-Culture* (Chicago: Haymarket Press, 2022).

2 Michael Brenes, "Joe Biden personifies Democratic Party failures since the Cold War," *The Nation* (March 11, 2020), Online: https://www.thenation.com/article/politics/cold-war-liberals-biden/

3 Jon Schwarz, "Everything Democrats didn't do in 2021," *The Intercept* (December 31, 2021). Online: https://theintercept.com/2021/12/31/democrats-biden-2021-failures/

4 Natasha Leonard, "Democrats' cowardice and complicity in the post-Roe world," *The Intercept* (July 5, 2022). Online: https://theintercept.com/2022/07/05/roe-wade-abortion-democrats-planned-parenthood/

5 Stanley Aronowitz, *Left Turn: Forging a New Political Future* (New York: Routledge, 2006). Liberals such as Thom Hartmann are convinced that real change will come from leftists and radicals working within the Democratic Party to change it. That position vastly underestimates their investment in neoliberalism, the market, and their long history of disdain for economic rights. The current crop of left-oriented politicians in the Democratic Party may get mainstream press coverage, but they are raging against a liberal centrist machine that treats them as the embarrassing uncle at the family reunion. See Thom Hartmann, "Why don't more progressives get that seizing the Democratic Party is our best chance to power?" The Hartmann Report (March 24, 2022). Online: https://mail.google.com/mail/u/0/#search/The+Hartmann+Report+/WhctKKXPknqRKSSRZjXTgMHctMRzblRmTMLzHdFVPpkt XKbqPzTHlzRvlNKHkGwwBfcppJb

6 Editorial, "Refuse fascism mission statement," *Refuse Fascism* (July 2021). Online: https://refusefascism.org/

7 Paul Street, "Why Biden may be less evil than Obama and Clinton—and why this may not matter all that much in the end," *Counterpunch* (January 22, 2021). Online: https://www.counterpunch.org/2021/01/22/why-biden-may-be-less-evil-than-obama-and-clinton-and-why-this-may-not-matter-all-that-much-in-the-end/

8 Paul Street, "No Joe: On character, quality and authenticity," *Counterpunch* (September 6, 2019). Online: https://www.counterpunch.org/2019/09/06/no-joe-on-character-quality-and-authenticity/

9 Richard D. Wolff, "The American political process is disconnected from economic reality," *Mail and Guardian* (February 25, 2022). Online: https://mg.co.za/article/2022-02-25-the-american-political-process-is-disconnected-from-economic-reality/

10 See: "Our demands," Poor People's Campaign (2022). Online: https://www.poorpeoplescampaign.org/about/our-demands/

11 Jason Pramas, "We need a mass left protest movement," *Counterpunch* (February 25, 2022). Online: https://www.counterpunch.org/2022/02/25/we-need-a-mass-left-protest-movement/

12 Ibid.

13 Ibid.

14 Zoe Williams, "The Saturday interview: Stuart Hall," *The Guardian* (February 11, 2012) http://www.guardian.co.uk/theguardian/2012/feb/11/saturday-interview-stuart-hall

15 Pankaj Mishra, "A Gandhian stand against the culture of cruelty," *The New York Review of Books*, [May 22, 2018]. Online: http://www.nybooks.com/daily/2018/05/22/the-culture-of-cruelty/

16 Howard Zinn, *People's History of the United States* (New York: Harper Collins Publisher, 1980/2010), p. 634.

17 James Baldwin, "As much truth as one can bear," *New York Times* (January 14, 1962), p. 38.

INDEX